Valentine's Dinner, Opolo Winery, February 14, 2007

Acknowledgements

There are countless people to thank and a lot of history behind this project. First and foremost our families and friends who have always been there for us to help with everything, no matter how involved or menial the job. Every member of our families brings an element of expertise to the table or they have been willing to be a quick study. If not for an amazing team of employees, some of whom have been with us for the entire 16 years, we wouldn't have had a chance. We know from personal experience that food service is hard work and requires a special personality and work ethic to make things run smoothly and successfully.

Thanks to Ron Bez who took the majority of the photographs in this book, and did a fabulous job. Thank you to Janice Solomon-Webb who worked above and beyond expectations on this book's beautiful design. Thanks to Tass Jones (Tass Jones Photography) for hanging out and shooting all the candids. A special thank you to Katy Budge for her help with editing, copywriting, photography and for helping me remain sane on those days I thought I would run away screaming. A big thank you to all the recipe testers whose experience or lack thereof helped to finalize recipes. What a team! You are all awesome, thanks so much!

Lisa & Jim

ISBN 978-0-9795082-0-2

Published in 2007
by Cahoots Publishing, a division of
Cahoots Catering Company
179 Niblick Road, Suite 202
Paso Robles, CA 93446,
www.cahootscatering.com.

Printed in the U. S. A.

CAHOOTS COOKBOOK

Recipes from the Central Coast's Premier Catering Company
Paso Robles, California

By Lisa Jones & Jim Subject

Contents

Foreword

On the prep table in the kitchen rested an opened book of handwritten recipes. The book was one of those journals you find in a stationery store, with different colored pages, a canvas cover, and a ribbon attached as the book mark. The corners were frayed; the canvas was faded and a bit sticky. It seemed as if it had been dusted with flour and patted off. This treasure held the recipes of Cahoots Catering Company, and some of them have made the journey into the pages of this cookbook.

I have so many fond memories of great meals from Lisa and Jim. I will never forget the aromas of grilled tri-tip, Citrus & Chardonnay Marinated Turkey, and sticky falling-off-the-bone ribs from the grill. How could I ignore the smell of the clam chowder simmering on the stove and the aroma of caramelized cheese from the "cheezy garlic bread" in the toaster? Both these talented chefs have sophisticated paletes with a casual approach. They have a way of making something as simple as a grilled ham and Swiss "the best I've ever had" because of grilled red onions and an easy mix of Dijon and mayonnaise.

When patrons entered Cahoots they didn't need a menu – they already knew what they wanted. Every guest had their "usual" that they would order time and time again. I especially remember Thursdays at Cahoots. It was the only day the "Thai Chicken Salad" was offered (because it required special preparation), and by 1 p.m. they were always sold out. That is the sort of passion and dedication that Lisa and Jim inspire in their patrons and their co-workers.

I have been involved with food for many years, beginning as a cook and server at Lisa and Jim's "Cahoots Catering Company & Café" in downtown Paso Robles. In fact, it was working there and seeing their enthusiasm and love for cooking that inspired me to become a chef. I attended the California Culinary Academy in San Francisco, and traveled and worked in many different establishments as a cook, server, and then finally a chef. I have studied various cuisines, and continue to learn about food, wine and dining. I've worked throughout the United States and the Caribbean at high-end restaurants and hotels, yet I continue to use the techniques, recipes and philosophies that I learned from Lisa and Jim. There is nothing that calls me home more than Lisa's cooking. She is, and always will be, my mentor.

As I write this forward to their book my mouth is starting to water. The recipes in this book are tried and true favorites, and have been developed with great thought and enthusiasm. Enjoy and savor this cookbook.

Happy Eating!
Chef Kelly Wangard

Kelly Wangard is a graduate of the California Culinary Academy in San Francisco and has served as executive chef at Loews Beverly Hills Hotel.

Introduction

It's an interesting life we live. A casual barbeque for 50...in the rain.
A five-course, plated sit-down winemaker dinner for 200...on a blustery
mountaintop. Preparing coffee at 4:00 in the morning to breathe life into 150
cowboys...out on the trail. Feeding nearly 1,000 Paso Robles Wine Festival
participants...from a tent in triple digit temperatures. Delighting a hostess
and eight of her closest friends...on New Year's Eve. It can be very rewarding
and challenging, exhausting and exhilarating all at the same time.

We are beginning our 16th year in business. After 12 years in our downtown
Paso Robles café and catering location, we are now continuing the catering
business from our licensed commissary kitchen located on our family ranch.
We are constantly asked if we will reopen the café portion of the business,
but – while we appreciate the support – quite frankly there's just not enough
of us to go around. We realized early on in our company that we had built
two businesses and we needed to choose one.

Our company continues to grow year after year. We feel privileged to have
the opportunity to work in such a wonderful community and grow alongside
the booming wine industry. When I moved to Paso Robles in 1982, there was
just a handful of wineries. Now in 2007, there are well over 125, and we have
developed a fantastic and fun relationship with many of them.

My husband Jim and I have slightly different thoughts, opinions and
approaches concerning food. But if there is a secret to our success, it would
be a shared commitment to quality, consistency, dedication and hard work.
I suppose that is what makes us such a good team.

Jim graduated from Cal Poly Pomona with a degree in hotel restaurant
management. He worked in the college cafeteria feeding volumes of food
to the masses, 400 to 500 customers a day. Jim also worked for a successful
catering company in Santa Barbara. He was involved in all kinds of events,
large and small, as well as the daily operation of the restaurant.

Jim is quite an accomplished barbeque-er and I don't think anyone, anywhere
can beat his Prime Rib. He loves the catering atmosphere where he can visit
with the guests around the barbeque pit or schmooze them on the
serving line.

For me food is personal. Ever since I was a little girl, I have always had an interest in cooking. I am constantly challenged to create, perfect and execute new ideas, recipes and menus for our customers.

When I was a teenager in the late 70s in San Diego, I began working for The Perfect Pan, a cutting edge gourmet cookware store and cooking school. Believe me, those were the days my friends. The Cuisinart food processor had just been introduced, gourmet cooking at home was beginning an upward surge and the concept of cooking schools was very new and exciting.

George and Piret Munger – whom I call my mentors to this day – owned and operated The Perfect Pan, and gave me untold opportunities. I not only worked in the store itself, but also assisted the instructors in the cooking school. It was my good fortune to assist some of the greats: Diana Kennedy, Paula Wolfert, Jacques Pépin, and Marcella Hazan to name a few.

The next experience with the Mungers was Piret's, a European-style charcuterie, boulangerie, and patisserie. We were working on opening the second store when I moved out of town and headed north by way of Santa Barbara and the Santa Ynez Valley.

My time here in Paso Robles has mostly been spent in the restaurant business as chef, manager, co-owner, and caterer, or all of the above. I was encouraged along the way to open my own place, but felt at the time it was too soon.

In 1991, I met Jim when we were working at the Main Street Grill in Templeton, California. As we began sharing our lives, thoughts about food and dreams for the future, we discovered we shared similar backgrounds and business ideas. That same year, we decided to take the plunge and open Cahoots Catering Co. in downtown Paso Robles. One of the most frequently asked questions is "How did you come up with the name Cahoots?" Probably the easiest explanation is that when we worked together, we found ourselves collaborating on our future, and finally someone asked if we were "in cahoots." I guess you could say the rest is history.

One of the other questions we are often asked is "Are you going to write a cookbook?" Well, you're holding the answer to that in your hands.

"Our growth depends not on how many experiences we devour, but on how many we digest"

Ralph W. Sockman

CHAPTER ONE

STARTERS

Grilled Vegetable Antipasto

Jim and I got the idea for this recipe while traveling through the Tuscan region of Italy. This is a beautiful presentation that explodes with taste and texture. The combination of grilled and marinated vegetables, sliced and marinated cheeses and tapanade served with crostini is a truly satisfying experience. "Buon appetito"!

1 eggplant

2 zucchini

1 bunch asparagus

2 large Portobello mushrooms

1/2-3/4 cup extra virgin olive oil

salt and pepper

3 roasted bell peppers, peeled and seeded (1 each red, yellow and green)

1 cup marinated artichoke hearts, drained

1/4 cup sun-dried tomatoes in oil, sliced in half, drained

1/2 pound smoked Fontina, sliced

3/4 cup Marinated Feta & Olives (recipe page 160)

3/4 cup Marinated Fresh Mozzarella (recipe page 161)

3/4 cup Tapanade (recipe page 156)

Fresh greens, such as arugula or herb salad greens, rinsed

1/4 cup each extra virgin olive oil and balsamic vinegar

1. Prepare a ridged grill pan over medium high heat or gas or charcoal grill.

2. Slice eggplant horizontally about 1/2-inch thick. Cut zucchini into 2-inch pieces, then cut each section into six wedges. Trim the stems off the asparagus, about the bottom 2 inches. After trimming the stems off the Portobello mushrooms, slice into 1/2-inch pieces. Brush or toss all vegetables with olive oil (reserving 2 tablespoons), salt and pepper.

3. Grill eggplant, zucchini, asparagus and mushrooms until just tender, being careful not to overcook or burn them.

4. Slice the roasted peppers into 1/2-inch thick strips; combine with reserved olive oil. Mix artichoke hearts and sun-dried tomatoes.

5. To serve: on an oval platter, pile a few handfuls of lettuce in the center, letting it cascade to the sides. Starting at one end lay out the eggplant, followed by the roasted peppers, the zucchini, the artichoke mixture, grilled Portobello mushrooms, and grilled asparagus, giving each equal distance around the outside edge.

6. In the center of the lettuce, arrange slices of Fontina cheese. On one side of the Fontina, pile on the marinated mozzarella, and on the other side, the marinated feta and olives.

7. Divide heaping spoonfuls of tapanade around the outside of the platter. Drizzle with extra virgin olive oil, balsamic vinegar, salt and fresh ground pepper. Serve with crackers, crostini or sliced baguettes.

Serves 10 -12

CHAPTER ONE • STARTERS

ADVANCE PREPARATION:
Can be made through step 5;
refrigerate and assemble 1 hour
before serving

WINE SUGGESTION:
A California Pinot Grigio,
Sangiovese or even a light-
bodied Syrah

Bruschetta with Trio of Spreads

Bruschetta comes from the Italian "bruscare," meaning "to roast over coals." Traditionally these bread slices are rubbed with fresh garlic, drizzled with extra virgin olive oil, salt and pepper and grilled over hot coals. I sometimes cheat and bake them in the oven or use a grill pan.

1 French baguette, sliced vertically in 1/2-inch pieces

2 large cloves garlic

1/4 cup extra virgin olive oil

SPREADS
1 cup Tapanade (recipe page 156)

Tuscan White Bean & Basil Spread (recipe page 15)

Goat Cheese, Fennel Pollen, Lavender & Pistachio Spread (recipe follows)

10 ounces goat cheese, softened

1/2 cup unsalted butter, softened

1/4 cup pistachios, lightly toasted

1 clove garlic, minced

1/2 teaspoon salt

1/2 teaspoon fennel pollen*

1/2 teaspoon dried lavender flowers

1. Prepare a charcoal or gas grill or heat a grill pan on the stove top.

2. Grill the slices of bread for about 1-2 minutes per side, until golden brown and marked by the grill. Arrange on a work surface and brush or drizzle with olive oil and then rub each bread slice with garlic.

3. Arrange your spreads in three serving dishes on a platter. Surround them with bruschetta and serve. *Serves 10-12*

Goat Cheese, Fennel Pollen, Lavender & Pistachio Spread

*Fennel Pollen was originally used as a seasoning by Italian chefs. Unlike the fennel seed, which is typically crushed to get at its flavor, fennel pollen is ready-to-use and provides nuanced levels of flavor – almost akin to a curry – with some of the same anise properties of fennel. Although the cost is a bit high, a little goes a long, long way. It is available at specialty food stores or your local health food store.

1. Add all ingredients to the work bowl of the food processor and pulse until blended.

14

Tuscan White Bean & Basil Spread

2 cloves garlic, minced

2, 15-1/2 ounce cans white beans, drained and rinsed

1/4 cup pine nuts, lightly toasted

1/3 cup Parmesan cheese, grated

1 tablespoon white balsamic vinegar

1 tablespoon lemon juice

1 teaspoon salt

1/2 teaspoon ground black pepper

1/4 teaspoon crushed red pepper

1/2 cup fresh basil leaves, torn into small pieces

3/4 cup extra virgin olive oil

1. Add all the ingredients to the work bowl of a food processor fitted with the steel blade. Pulse processor, on and off for about 30 seconds until blended.

ADVANCE PREPARATION:
All spreads can be made the night before. Refrigerate until ready to use. Bring goat cheese spread to room temperature before serving.

WINE SUGGESTION:
A full-bodied Chardonnay or Pinot Noir

Seed Crusted Seared Ahi on a Won Ton Crisp with Asian Slaw & Wasabi Aioli

This is an amazing blend of flavors. The wonderful combination of toasted seeds, the Asian vinaigrette on the slaw and wasabi aioli all on a crunchy won-ton crisp is magical. If you are a little squeamish about rare Ahi, this dish could very well change your mind.

12 won ton wrappers

1/2 cup vegetable oil

1 cup Asian Slaw, omit the cashews (recipe page 54)

**Wasabi Aioli
(recipe page 163)**

1/2 pound good quality ahi, about 1 steak, 1-inch thick

2 teaspoons mustard seeds

1 tablespoon sesame seeds

2 teaspoons poppy seeds

salt & pepper

1 tablespoon olive oil

cilantro leaves for garnish

HELPFUL HINT: A resealable plastic bag with a corner snipped off can be used in place of a pastry bag.

1. In a frying pan, heat vegetable oil over medium high heat. While the oil is heating, cut the won ton wrappers in half on the diagonal. Carefully fry in small batches until light brown and crisp, remove and drain. Take care not to burn as they cook quickly. Store in an air-tight container until ready to use or for up to 2 days.

2. Prepare the Asian slaw, omitting the cashews.

3. Prepare the wasabi aioli.

4. Mix the seeds and pepper together in a small bowl. Coat ahi on all sides with olive oil. Lightly sprinkle with salt. Generously coat the ahi in the seed mixture on all sides.

5. Heat a medium-sized sauté pan over high heat. When the pan is hot add the ahi. Sear the ahi for about 3 minutes per side. Remove from heat and set aside. When cool enough to handle, slice into thin slices, approximately 1/4- inch thick and 1-1/2 inches long.

6. To assemble, spread the won ton crisps on a serving platter. Using a pastry bag with a small round tip, pipe a dollop of wasabi aioli (about a 1/2 teaspoon) onto each won ton Top with a slice of ahi. Top with a generous tablespoon of Asian slaw. Top the slaw with another dollop of wasabi aioli, about 1/4 teaspoon. Garnish with cilantro leaf.
Serves 4-6

WINE SUGGESTION:
Viognier or Roussanne

Camarones en Escabeche

"Escabeche" is a term used for poached or fried fish, covered in a spicy marinade for at least 24 hours. This dish will fool you; it seems as if it would be very spicy but the flavor is actually fairly tame. This is a refreshing and delicious dish to serve on a hot summer evening.

1 pound shrimp (16-20 count)*

1/2 cup white onion, chopped

2 cloves garlic, chopped

1/2 cup olive oil, divided

1/4 cup red wine vinegar

1/2 teaspoon salt

1/4 cup marinade from a can of jalapeños en escabeche**

1/2 cup green onions, chopped

1 Serrano chile, thinly sliced

1/2 cup Zanajorias en Escabeche (Marinated sliced carrots)*, drained**

1/4 cup cilantro, chopped, for garnish

*NOTE: *Shrimp is generally sold by size and weight so if you purchase 16/20 shrimp that means there are approximately 16 to 20 shrimp per pound. I was told by my fish monger that 16/20 shrimp and above are considered prawns.*
***You can reserve the jalapeños for another use, such as in the Southwestern Frittata with Chorizo, page 77.*
**** Available in most stores near the canned jalapeños*

1. Heat 1/4 cup of olive oil in a sauté pan. Add onions, garlic, sauté for about a minute. Add shrimp. Cook until the shrimp are pink and cooked through, about 3 minutes.

2. Remove the shrimp from the heat, drain and place in a medium stainless or glass bowl. Add the remaining 1/4 cup of olive oil, vinegar, salt, jalapeño marinade, green onions, Serrano chile and marinated sliced carrots. Marinate overnight in the refrigerator.

3. To serve, drain off half the marinade and transfer to a serving bowl. Garnish with chopped cilantro.
Serves 4-6

WINE SUGGESTION:
Albariño or light-bodied, food-friendly Zinfandel

Cahoots Gourmet Cheese Roll

We have made this recipe from the very beginning and it is always a winner. All these years people have asked me what kind of cheeses are in it and I have always been vague about the description, partly because of the simplicity of the ingredients. Originally when we started making this we layered it, which you can do, but I found this method to be much easier.

1 pound cream cheese, softened

1/2 pound unsalted butter, softened

1/2 cup basil pesto (recipe page 155)

1/2 cup tapanade (recipe page 156)

1/2 cup sun-dried tomato pesto (recipe page 156)

1. Using a hand mixer, blend the cream cheese and butter together. Take a jelly roll pan and line it with a sheet of plastic wrap, leaving a 1-inch overhang on one of the long sides. Spread the cheese mixture onto the plastic wrap about 1/2 inch thick and about 8x10 inches.

2. Spread the basil pesto on the top one-third of the long side of the cheese mixture. Spread the sun dried tomato pesto on the middle third of the mixture. Spread the tapanade on the bottom third of the cheese mixture. Chill until it begins to firm up but is still pliable, about 15 minutes.

3. Carefully take the over-hanging edge of the plastic wrap and begin to roll jelly roll style, using the plastic as an aid and keeping it on the outside of the roll. Once it is rolled refrigerate until firm, at least an hour.

4. To serve, remove plastic wrap. Trim the ends of the roll and serve with crackers, crostini or sliced baguettes.
    Serves 10-12

ADVANCE PREPARATION:
Can be made up to 24 hours in advance.

Marinated Mozzarella, Tomato & Basil with Pesto Drizzle

This is a very popular selection on our catering menu, and makes for an easy-to-prepare, but stunning presentation. Fresh Mozzarella comes in many sizes. What seems to work best for this recipe are the bocconcini (also called "cherry size") or 4-ounce balls cut into 10-12 pieces.

1/2 pound marinated bocconcini mozzarella (recipe page 161)

20 cherry tomatoes, preferably mixed heirlooms

20 small basil leaves

2 tablespoons basil pesto (recipe page155)

2 tablespoons extra virgin olive oil

20 4-inch skewers

1. Skewer one mozzarella ball, then one basil leaf, then one cherry tomato. Arrange on a platter mixing the colors if using heirloom or mixed color cherry tomatoes.

2. Whisk basil pesto with olive oil. Drizzle over the top of the skewers and serve.
   Serves 6-8

Southwestern Black Bean Torte

This is very fun and festive and can be done ahead. With so many layers of flavors, this dish takes you by surprise with all its different textures and tastes. This can be served with crackers, pita crisps or tortilla chips.

3 cups Cahoots black beans (recipe page 89)

Cilantro pesto (recipe page 155)

5 mild whole green chilies, fresh or canned, roasted, peeled and seeded

2 roasted bell peppers, preferably 1 red and 1 yellow, fresh or canned, roasted, peeled and seeded

1 cup feta cheese, crumbled

1/2 cup sour cream

1. Line a 4" x 8" loaf pan with plastic wrap leaving a 2-inch overhang on all sides. Spread 1 cup of the black beans in the bottom of the pan in a smooth layer.

2. Spread 1/2 cup cilantro pesto over the bean mixture.

3. Dice the green chiles and the roasted red peppers and mix together. Set aside 1/4 cup for garnish. Sprinkle the rest of the pepper mixture over the pesto.

4. Top the peppers with a layer of crumbled feta cheese. Top the feta with the remaining black beans, gently pressing.

5. Cover the loaf with the overhanging plastic wrap and let chill for about 2 hours or overnight.

6. To serve, peel back plastic from top of loaf pan. Place serving dish upside down on the loaf pan. Holding both the loaf pan and the serving dish, invert them. Carefully peel away the plastic wrap.

7. Mix sour cream with the remaining 1/4 cup of pesto. Drizzle over the top. Finish with the remaining diced peppers.
Serves 10-12

WINE SUGGESTION:
Albariño or Zinfandel
(or a crisp, cold Mexican beer)

Grilled Citrus, Herb & Garlic Prawns

You can't eat just one! This is very yummy, so plan accordingly. We placed this recipe in the appetizer section, but you can make a meal of it. Don't be afraid of the amount of garlic-it's great.

1/3 cup garlic, chopped in the food processor with 2 teaspoons salt

Zest from 1 lemon, 1 lime and 1 orange

1 tablespoon fresh rosemary, minced

1 tablespoon fresh cilantro leaves, roughly chopped

1/2 cup extra virgin olive oil

2 pounds 16/20 count shrimp, peeled, deveined, tails on

6 10-inch wooden skewers, soaked in water

Rosemary sprigs

Chopped cilantro for garnish

1. In a bowl mix together garlic, salt, zest, rosemary, cilantro, and olive oil. Add shrimp. Mix well and marinate in the refrigerator at least 4 to 6 hours.

2. Prepare the charcoal or gas grill, or ridged grill pan.

3. Thread shrimp onto the skewers, first through the top of the shrimp and then again just above the tail, about 6 per skewer.

4. Grill shrimp for about 3 to 4 minutes per side or until just done, pink and opaque.

5. To serve, garnish a platter with rosemary sprigs. Remove shrimp from the skewers, scatter over the rosemary. Top with chopped cilantro.
Serves 4-6

WINE SUGGESTION:
Pinot Blanc or light-bodied red
Rhône blend

Assorted Flatbread Pizzas

Maytag blue cheese, shiitake mushroom & smoked chicken, Marinated feta cheese & basil pesto, Sun-dried tomato, goat cheese & arugula.

This is a great party appetizer because it can be almost entirely prepared ahead so as your guests arrive you can pop them in the oven as you need them. This is also fun if you like interactive cooking parties. Have your flatbread and toppings prepared ahead and encourage your guests to make their own pizzas. There are no rules here; feel free to create your own concoctions.

3, 12-ounce packages purchased pizza dough

2 tablespoons unsalted butter

2 cloves garlic, minced

1/2 pound shiitake mushrooms, (approx. 4 cups before stemmed and sliced) stemmed and sliced

1/4 cup extra virgin olive oil

1/2 cup basil pesto (recipe page155)

1 pound (approx. 4 cups) grated mozzarella

1/2 pound smoked or grilled chicken breast, shredded

1 cup Maytag blue cheese or other blue cheese, crumbled

1 cup marinated feta and olives (recipe page 160)

1 cup arugula, coarsely chopped

3 cloves garlic, chopped

1 cup sun dried tomatoes in oil, coarsely chopped

8 ounces goat cheese, crumbled

1/4 cup grated Parmesan cheese

salt and pepper to taste

1. Preheat oven to 400 degrees F.

2. Roll out pizza dough and place each dough on a separate baking pan. Prebake the doughs for 6 minutes.

3. Melt butter in a small sauté pan over medium high heat. Add garlic and cook for 1 minute. Add mushrooms and continue cooking for another 2 minutes until soft, remove from heat.

4. Brush two of the three crusts with olive oil. Spread the basil pesto over the third crust.

5. Divide the mozzarella between the three crusts, reserving 1-1/2 cups for the tops.

6. On one of the oiled crusts with cheese, add sautéed mushrooms, shredded chicken, blue cheese and an additional 1/2 cup grated mozzarella.

7. On the crust with basil pesto top with marinated feta & olives and an additional 1/2 cup of mozzarella cheese.

8. On the remaining crust with olive oil and cheese, add chopped arugula, garlic, sun dried tomatoes, goat cheese and an additional 1/2 cup of grated mozzarella.

9. Top all three pizzas with Parmesan cheese. Sprinkle all three pizzas with salt and pepper to taste. Bake for 8-10 minutes until golden brown and bubbly. Cut into squares or wedges and serve.
Serves 10-12, or makes 36 3-inch squares

NOTE: Maytag blue cheese is a Roquefort-style blue cheese. This cheese was developed by Fred Maytag II, yes the same guy that brought us the washing machine.

WINE SUGGESTION:
Mourvèdre (especially with the mushroom pizza) or Cabernet Sauvignon

Barbequed Oysters with Three Dipping Sauces

We cook thousands of oysters a year at Tobin James Cellars for their annual barbeques in the early summer and early fall. Not surprisingly, people love them! In addition to the standard accompaniments, we also serve these three sauces. I like to let the oysters open on the grill. Shellfish, such as oysters, mussels and clams – have fresh bivalves that pop open when they are cooked. Be sure to discard any that do not open.

24 fresh oysters (we like "Fanny Bay") scrub away any mud and rinse but do not submerse in water.

4 cups coarse salt

CAHOOTS OYSTER BASTE (recipe page 28)

COCONUT LIME SAUCE (recipe page 28)

TATAKI SAUCE (recipe page 29)

HORSERADISH SALSA FRESCA (recipe page 29)

HELPFUL HINT: I like to add a variety of spices to the coarse salt used to keep the oysters in place; not only is it visually appealing, it is also very aromatic when the hot oyster shells hit the salt. This is also a great opportunity to clean out your spice cupboard of those odd spices that have been there for too long.

1. Prepare a charcoal or gas grill.

2. Have the Cahoots Oyster Baste and dipping sauces ready to go before you start grilling the oysters. Place unopened oysters on the grill, flat side up.

3. Grill oysters over medium high heat until they begin opening. Once they open, carefully remove them from the grill and set on a folded towel. Remove the lid (top shell) by cutting the attaching muscle away from the shell, being careful not to spill out any of the oyster liquor (the liquid surrounding the oyster).

4. Return oysters to grill and spoon the oyster baste over them, about one tablespoon, depending on the size of the oyster. Because of the oils and butter in the oyster baste, be very careful of possible flame-ups from the grill when you baste the oysters. Grill the oysters for about 3-4 minutes until the oyster baste begins to bubble.

5. Pour the coarse salt onto a serving platter to help hold the oysters in place. Remove oysters from grill and place on the serving platter and serve with dipping sauces.
Serves 6-8

Wine suggestion:
Champagne or sparkling wine
or Sauvignon Blanc

27

Cahoots Oyster Baste

1/2 pound butter

4 tablespoons lemon juice

1 tablespoon Cahoots House Rub or other all purpose seasoning

3 cloves garlic, finely chopped

1. In a small saucepan melt butter. Add lemon juice, seasoning and garlic. Let simmer over low heat for about 5-7 minutes. Can be made ahead, refrigerated and rewarmed.

Coconut Lime Sauce

2 tablespoons corn oil

2 cloves garlic, chopped

1 shallot, chopped

1 1-ounce package lemon grass, chopped

1 knob of ginger, chopped (about 1-2 tablespoons)

1/2 cup seasoned rice wine vinegar

8 ounces coconut milk

1 teaspoon garlic chili sauce

1 tablepoon cilantro, chopped

Juice of 2 limes

1. Sauté garlic, shallot, lemon grass, and ginger in oil until shallots are soft and have no color.

2. Add vinegar and simmer gently until reduced by half. Add coconut milk and reduce again by half until thick.

3. Cool to room temperature; strain. Add garlic chili sauce, cilantro and lime juice.

Tataki Sauce

1/3 cup low sodium soy sauce

1/4 cup seasoned rice wine vinegar

1 tablespoon olive oil

3 green onions, thinly sliced

2 cloves garlic, minced

1 tablespoon lemon juice

1 tablespoon lime juice

1/2 teaspoon ground ginger

1. Mix all ingredients together.

Horseradish Salsa Fresca

2 medium tomatoes, chopped

1/4 cup white onion, chopped

1 jalapeño chile, seeded and chopped

2 tablespoons cilantro, chopped

1 teaspoon prepared horseradish

1/2 teaspoon kosher salt

1. Mix all ingredients together.

CHAPTER TWO

Soups

Roasted Butternut Squash Soup

This is a simple soup to make. In the fall I start craving winter squashes – whether they are in a soup, ravioli or a pie, I get the urge. We have served this soup (as well as the Pumpkin Corn Chowder page 43) at the J. Lohr Wine Center for their fall open house, and we had so many requests for the recipe we agreed to publish it in their newsletter. I like to serve it as an appetizer in a little teacup or demitasse cup as guests arrive; it helps "break the ice."

1 head of garlic, trim top and peel off loose outer skin

1 onion, unpeeled and quartered

2 pounds butternut squash (about 1 squash), carefully cut into 8 pieces, seeds removed

1/4 cup olive oil

salt and pepper to taste

2 teaspoons fresh thyme

1/2 cup cream

1-3/4 cups chicken stock, warmed (recipe page 157)

1. Preheat oven to 325 degrees F (300 degrees convection).

2. Place the garlic, onion and butternut squash on a baking sheet. Drizzle with olive oil and season with salt, pepper and thyme. Bake for about 60 minutes or until tender.

3. Scrape squash off the skin, discard skin. Peel the onion and squeeze garlic cloves out of their skin. Puree in food processor with pan juices. Add puree to a 4-quart saucepan.

4. Warm pan with puree over medium heat. Add cream and whisk in warmed chicken stock. Heat through. Season with salt and pepper.
    Serves 6-8

HELPFUL HINT: Be very careful when you cut up the butternut squash, as they can get away from you. The skins are hard to cut and they roll. They are also very easy to grow in your garden and hold well through the winter.

White Gazpacho

This is one of our personal favorites. When we first started serving it in the restaurant we had plenty of skeptics. We added this cold refreshing soup to our Wine Festival menu and we have returning customers who stop by every year for a bowl. The hardest part is keeping the staff (myself included) out of it. I find this soup to be a perfect summer soup, best when the tomatoes are vine ripened and served ice cold on a hot summer day.

3 cucumbers (preferably English or hot house), peeled

4 tomatoes, chopped

1/2 cup green onions, thinly sliced

1/2 cup fresh parsley, chopped

3 cloves garlic, finely chopped

2 cups sour cream

1 cup yogurt

1 cup chicken (recipe page 157) or vegetable broth

3 tablespoons red wine vinegar

juice of 1 lemon

1-1/2 teaspoons salt

1 teaspoon ground white pepper

1 cup sunflower seeds, toasted and salted, for garnish

1. Dice one of the cucumbers and add to a bowl along with the chopped tomatoes, green onions, parsley and garlic.

2. Cut the remaining two cucumbers into one-inch cubes.

3. In the food processor or blender, add one half of the cucumber pieces and puree with the sour cream until smooth. Add to the bowl of vegetables. Repeat this step with the other half of the cucumber pieces and the yogurt. Add to the bowl of vegetables.

4. Add the chicken or vegetable stock, red wine vinegar, lemon juice, salt and white pepper. Stir well and chill for about 2 hours.

5. To serve, top with sunflower seeds.
   Serves 6-8.

HELPFUL HINT: This soup can be made with low-fat, non-fat or light sour cream and yogurt; however it does change the flavor. In my opinion it's worth the calories to try this version.

34

Cahoots Clam Chowder

Our clam chowder was so popular we served it everyday in the restaurant instead of Friday only. In the winter months when it was cold and rainy, we couldn't seem to make enough of it and in the summer when it was well over 100 degrees outside it was still a big seller. A favorite selection was the "Cahootful" – a hollowed-out sourdough bread bowl filled with the chowder.

2 slices uncooked thick sliced bacon

2 Russet potatoes, washed, diced into 1/2-inch cubes

1 large red onion, chopped

5 stalks celery, chopped

1 large carrot, diced

1-1/2 cups clam juice

2, 15-ounce cans chopped clams

1 tablespoon salt

2 teaspoons ground black pepper

1/4 teaspoon ground allspice

3 dashes of hot sauce

1 quart (4 cups) half & half

8 tablespoons (1 stick) of unsalted butter

3/4 cup flour

1. Chop bacon into 1/2-inch pieces. Add to 8-quart stockpot or saucepan. Cook over medium heat stirring often, to render (melt the fat), and the bacon begins to crisp. Be careful not to burn the bacon, as it will make your soup very dark and unpleasant.

2. When bacon is rendered add the chopped onion and stir well. Then add potatoes, stir again and let cook for about 2-3 minutes, stirring occasionally. Add celery, carrot, clam juice, clams, salt, pepper, allspice and hot sauce. Let simmer for 15 to 20 minutes until the vegetables are soft.

3. Add half & half. Let the chowder come up to a simmer over medium heat without boiling.

4. While the chowder is heating melt butter in a small saucepan over medium heat. Add flour and whisk together. This mixture is known as "a roux." Cook the roux until it turns a light beige color and the raw flour smell is gone, about 5 minutes.

5. When the chowder is hot whisk the roux into the chowder, making sure there are no lumps of roux, and whisk until thickened.
Serves 6-8

Tomato Bisque

This is one of Jim's favorite soups. He likes it with a grilled cheese sandwich and a glass of milk. Feel free to substitute chicken or vegetable broth in place of the clam juice. You can dress-up this soup with some homemade cheesy croutons or crostinis floated on top.

3 slices uncooked thick sliced bacon

3 cloves garlic, minced

1 cup yellow onion, chopped

2 stalks celery, chopped, about 1 cup

2, 28-ounce cans chopped tomatoes

1 teaspoon salt

1 teaspoon Italian seasoning

1 teaspoon black pepper

1 teaspoon fennel seed, lightly crushed with the flat side of a knife blade or spice grinder

2 cups clam juice (or broth)

2 tablespoons unsalted butter

2 tablespoons flour

1/2 cup cream (or half & half)

1. Chop bacon into 1/2-inch pieces. Add to 6-quart stockpot or saucepan. Cook over medium heat stirring often, to render (melt) the fat and the bacon begins to crisp. Be careful not to burn the bacon.

2. When the bacon is rendered, add the garlic, onion, and celery. Stir often and let cook for about 3 minutes.

3. Add chopped tomatoes, salt, Italian seasoning, pepper, and fennel seed. Cover and let simmer for about 30 minutes.

4. Remove lid from pan and carefully puree the mixture with a hand-held immersion blender. (If you don't have an immersion blender you can use a regular blender but be very careful when blending hot liquids.) Blend in several batches until smooth, leaving plenty of room for expansion and covering the blender with a towel. Return to pan.

5. Add clam juice (or broth) and warm slowly until just about at boiling point.

6. While the soup is warming, melt butter in a small saucepan over medium heat. Add flour and whisk together to make a roux. Cook the roux until it turns a light beige color and the raw flour smell is gone, about 5 minutes.

7. When the soup is hot whisk the roux into the soup, making sure there are no lumps of roux, and whisk until thickened. Stir in cream and serve.
Serves 6-8

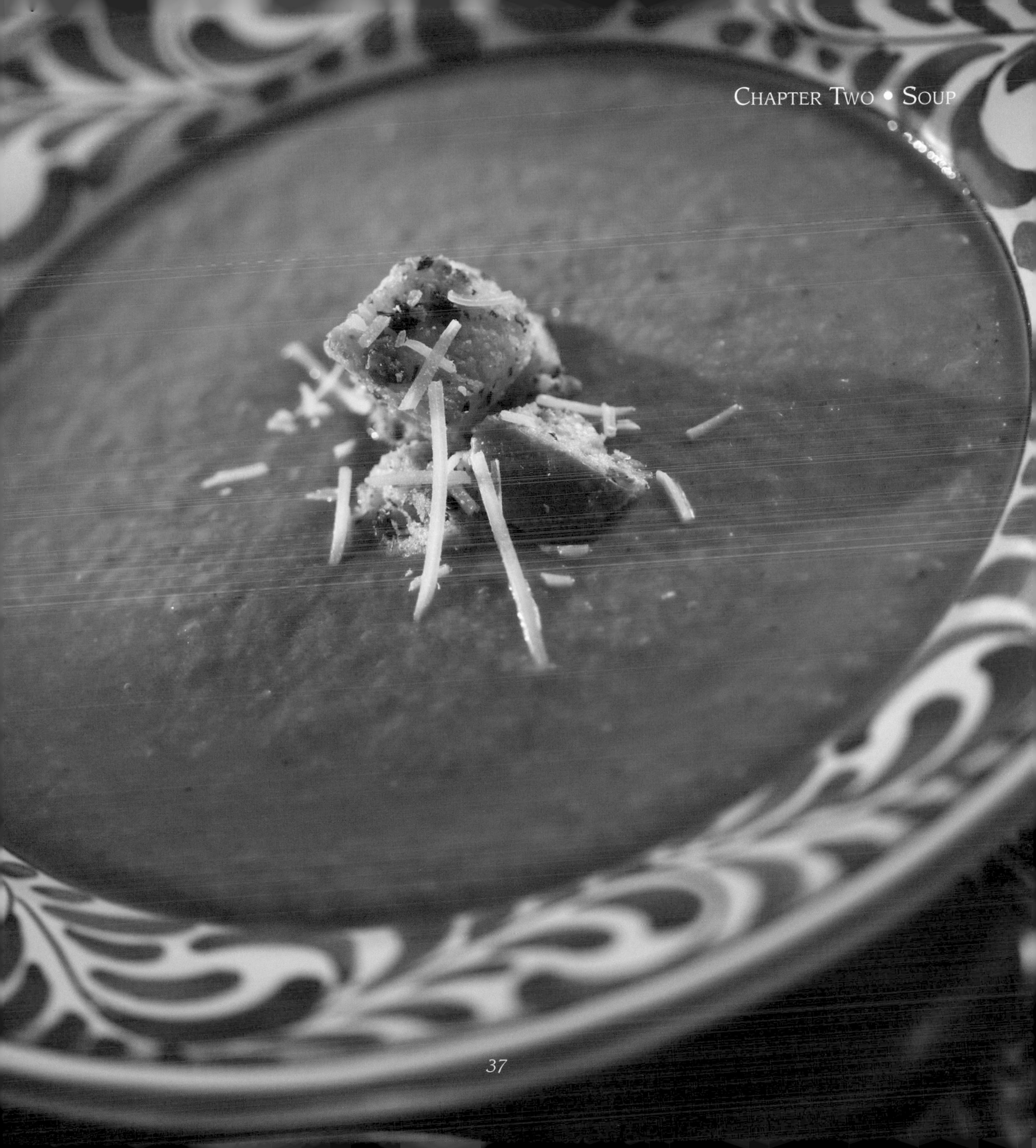

Potato Leek Soup

This is the ultimate "comfort soup." It's great on a bone-chilling cold day. It is like a baked potato with the works made into soup.

1/2 pound good quality bacon, diced

4 leeks, white and light green parts, sliced and rinsed (about 2 cups)

1 red onion chopped, about 1-1/2 cups

4 stalks celery, chopped

3 pounds Russet potatoes, scrubbed, not peeled, 1 grated, others diced

8 cups chicken stock (recipe page 157)

1 tablespoon dried parsley flakes

1 teaspoon dried thyme

2 teaspoons salt

1 teaspoon ground black pepper

1/4 cup unsalted butter

1/4 cup flour

8 ounces cream cheese, softened

2 cups half & half

1. In a medium stock pot cook the bacon over medium heat until it starts to crisp.

2. Add the leeks and onion; continue to cook over moderate heat for about 5 minutes stirring occasionally. Add celery, potatoes and stir until mixed. Add chicken stock, parsley flakes, thyme, salt and pepper. Cover and simmer for about 20 to 30 minutes until the potatoes are tender.

3. In a separate sauce pan melt butter, add flour and whisk together to make a roux. Cook the roux until it turns a light beige color and the raw flour smell is gone, about 5 minutes, then stir into soup. Whisk in softened cream cheese and half & half. Garnish if desired with chopped herbs.
Serves 8-10

HELPFUL HINT: The reason I grate one of the potatoes is to help thicken the soup.

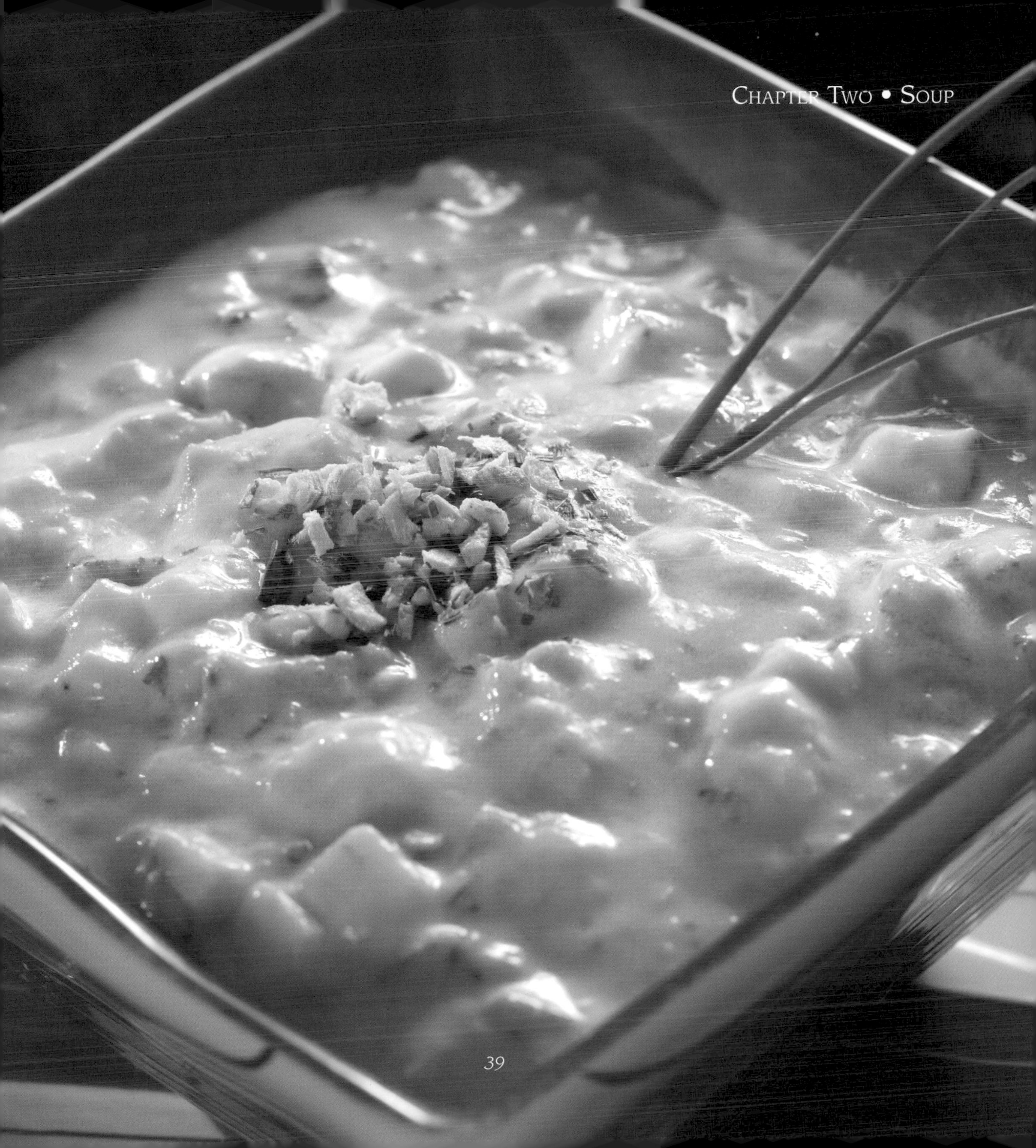

Hot & Sour Soup

This is an Asian-inspired recipe that also happens to be one of my favorite "chicken soups." If you're feeling a little under the weather this should fix you right up.

8 cups chicken stock (recipe page 157)

1/4 cup cornstarch

2 egg whites

4 cloves garlic, chopped

2-4 Serrano chilies, chopped

1 small head Napa cabbage, sliced

12-15 snow peas, strings removed and sliced in half

4 ounces sliced mushrooms, preferably shiitake

1 cup shredded cooked chicken

1/4 cup seasoned rice wine vinegar

2 tablespoons soy sauce

1 tablespoon sesame oil

5 green onions, thinly sliced

1. Whisk together 1/2 cup of the chicken stock with the cornstarch and set aside. In another bowl whisk egg whites until blended, set aside.

2. Bring remaining chicken stock to a boil in a 6 quart stock pot. Gradually add the cornstarch mixture, stir well. Slowly add egg whites in a continuous stream, stir well.

3. Add garlic, chilies, Napa cabbage, snow peas, mushrooms, chicken, rice vinegar, soy sauce, sesame oil and green onions. Reduce soup to a simmer. Cook for about 10 minutes and serve.
   Serves 6-8

Split Pea with Ham Soup

I was never much of a split pea soup person; however, this one I love, and all of our customers think this rich, delicious and rib-sticking soup is a real winner!

2 smoked ham shanks, (about 2 pounds)

2 tablespoons butter

1 cup onion, chopped

3 cloves garlic, chopped

2 carrots, peeled and chopped

2 Russet potatoes, washed and diced

7 cups chicken stock (recipe page 157)

1 pound dry split peas

1 teaspoons ground black pepper

1 cup milk

1. In a large stock pot, brown the ham shanks on all sides over medium-high heat, about 5 minutes. Add butter.

2. When the butter is melted add onion, garlic, carrots and potatoes. Cook until soft, about 4-5 minutes.

3. Add chicken stock, split peas and pepper. Reduce heat to low; cook uncovered for about 1 hour or until the meat is falling off the bones of the ham shanks.

4. Remove soup from heat. Using tongs or slotted spoon, carefully remove ham shanks from soup, making sure you don't leave any bones behind. Set shanks aside until they are cool enough to handle; remove the meat from the shanks and chop.

5. Add the meat back into the soup, stir in milk, gently warm until heated through.
Serves 6-8

Minestrone

This is a wonderful recipe if you have leftover vegetables, since you can add just about any combination. I like to finish this soup with fresh spinach just before I serve it and top each serving with a homemade crouton and grated Parmesan cheese.

2 slices uncooked bacon, chopped

1 onion, chopped

1/2 pound Italian sausage, cooked and drained

2 cloves garlic

1 tablespoon Italian Seasoning

2 tablespoons chopped parsley

1/4 teaspoon cayenne pepper

1/2 teaspoon black pepper

2 teaspoons salt

2 quarts beef stock

2 Russet potatoes, washed and diced

2, 15-1/2-ounce cans diced tomatoes, drained

1-1/2 cups assorted diced vegetables (carrots, green beans, corn etc.)

8 ounces pasta, appropriate for soup (small shell or macaroni)

5 ounces (about 4 cups) fresh baby spinach

1. Cook bacon in a stock pot over medium-high heat until it begins to crisp. Add onion, sausage, garlic, Italian seasoning, parsley, cayenne, pepper, salt, beef stock, and diced potatoes. Simmer until the potatoes are just tender, about 20 minutes.

2. Add assorted vegetables, tomatoes, and pasta. Cook until pasta is cooked, about an additional 12 minutes. Stir in fresh spinach, let simmer for a minute or two and serve.
   Serves 6-8

WINE SUGGESTION:
Any red Italian varietal such as a Nebbiolo

Pumpkin Corn Chowder

This soup is bursting with Fall flavor. It would make a beautiful first course for a Thanksgiving feast or a hearty one-bowl meal on a chilly evening.

1 tablespoon unsalted butter

2 cloves garlic, minced

1 onion, chopped

2 stalks celery, chopped

1 cup red bell pepper, chopped

1 small potato, diced

4 cups chicken stock (recipe page 157)

1, 16-ounce can pumpkin purée

1 cup corn kernels, fresh or frozen

1 teaspoon salt

1/2 teaspoon ground black pepper

1 teaspoon poultry seasoning

1. Melt butter in a medium saucepan. Add garlic and onion, sauté until soft, about 3 minutes.

2. Add celery, red bell pepper and potato, continue cooking for another 3 minutes stirring frequently.

3. Add chicken stock, pumpkin purée, corn, salt, pepper, and poultry seasoning.

4. Cover and simmer for 25 to 30 minutes until vegetables are tender.
Serves 6-8

CHAPTER THREE

SALADS

45

Pasta Salad with Fresh Baby Spinach & Feta

This is a very popular salad, so I expect to have some happy customers when they see this recipe. We served this in our restaurant every day and it was a staple for many of our customers. This is another versatile recipe, so you may choose to add toasted nuts, substitute different cheeses or use a different type of pasta. I personally like to replace the baby spinach with fresh baby arugula.

12 ounces small shell pasta

1 tablespoon vegetable oil plus 1 teaspoon salt for pasta water

3/4 cup olive oil

3/4 cup red wine vinegar

1-2 cloves of garlic, chopped (I use 2)

2 teaspoons Dijon mustard

2 teaspoons salt

1 teaspoon ground black pepper

2 tomatoes, chopped

1 cucumber, peeled and sliced

1/2 cup green onions, thinly sliced

1/2 cup Parmesan cheese, grated

4 ounces feta cheese, crumbled

12 ounces fresh baby spinach

1. Bring 4 quarts of water with vegetable oil and salt to a boil. Add pasta and cook until al dente, about 6-8 minutes. Drain.

2. In a large bowl whisk together olive oil, red wine vinegar, garlic, mustard, salt and pepper until well combined.

3. Add cooked pasta, stir well. Add chopped tomatoes, cucumber, green onions, Parmesan cheese, feta cheese and baby spinach. Toss well and serve.
   Makes 10-12 servings

HELPFUL HINT: "Al dente" is an Italian phrase that means "to the tooth" and refers to the texture of pasta when it is perfectly cooked. To test the pasta, just take a piece and bite into it; if it's slightly chewy with a bit of resistance in the center, it's al dente.

WINE SUGGESTION:
Any crisp white Rhône blend

Yukon Gold Potato Salad with Caramelized Leeks, Goat Cheese & Asparagus

This is a hit every year at Tobin James Cellars' annual "Not Your Average Backyard Barbeque" held every June at the winery. It's a great kick off to summer in the wine country. We usually serve about 400 people and a good time is had by all.

1 tablespoon olive oil

4 leeks, white and light green parts, thinly sliced and rinsed (about 2 cups)

4 pounds Yukon Gold potatoes,

3 stalks celery, rinsed, patted dry, chopped

1 pound fresh asparagus (about 1 bunch)

1/4 cup fresh tarragon, chopped

1/4 cup fresh chives, chopped

6 ounces goat cheese, crumbled

1 cup mayonnaise

1 tablespoon Dijon mustard

2 tablespoons apple cider vinegar

2 teaspoons salt

1 teaspoon ground black pepper

1. In an 8-quart saucepan or stock pot add the potatoes. Cover with water, bring to a boil and cook until tender when pierced with a knife.

2. In a small saucepan bring one quart of water to a boil. Cut the asparagus into 1-inch pieces. Add to the boiling water and blanch until just tender, about two minutes.

3. In a large sauté pan heat olive oil over medium low heat. Add sliced leeks and cook, stirring occasionally, until the leeks begin to brown lightly and caramelize. Set aside.

4. Cut cooked potatoes into 1-inch pieces and put into mixing bowl. Add celery, asparagus, tarragon, chives, goat cheese and caramelized leeks. Toss lightly to mix.

5. In a separate bowl, whisk together mayonnaise, Dijon, vinegar, salt and pepper. Pour over salad and toss until well mixed, but don't over mix.
Serves 12-14

Red Potato Salad

This recipe is so simple that when I tell people the ingredients they are certain I am leaving something out. If there is a secret it is marinating the chopped red onions in red wine vinegar. The beauty of this recipe is the simplicity, which allows you to add different herbs, or toasted nuts if you like. I started making this salad when I worked for Main St. Grill in Templeton, California, and at that time, I added lots of fresh dill.

1/2 large red onion, peeled and chopped

2 tablespoons red wine vinegar

3 pounds red potatoes

4 stalks celery, rinsed, patted dry, diced

1/2 teaspoon salt

1/2 teaspoon ground black pepper

1 cup mayonnaise

1. Add red potatoes to a 6-quart sauce pan. Cover with water and bring to a boil. Cook until tender when pierced with a knife.

2. Add chopped red onion to a small bowl. Add red wine vinegar, toss and let marinate for about 15 minutes.

3. Cut cooked red potatoes into one-inch pieces and put in mixing bowl.

4. Drain red wine vinegar from the red onions. To the cut potatoes add diced celery, drained red onions, salt, pepper and mix well. Add mayonnaise, mix to combine. Add any additional fresh herbs or 1/2 cup toasted nuts if you choose.
Makes 10-12 servings

Chicken Salad with Tarragon & Pine Nuts

This is a very versatile salad. We have served it in a sandwich, stuffed in a tomato, over sliced avocado and in a tortilla wrap. It has great balance of taste and texture.

1 pound cooked chicken breast, finely chopped

2 stalks celery, finely chopped

3 green onions, finely chopped

2 tablespoons fresh tarragon, finely chopped

3 tablespoons pine nuts, lightly toasted and coarsely chopped

3/4 cup mayonnaise

1 teaspoon Dijon mustard

1 teaspoon lemon juice

1/4 teaspoon salt

1/4 teaspoon ground black pepper

1. Add all ingredients to a bowl and mix well.
   Serves 6-8

HELPFUL HINT: Toasting nuts ... sounds easy enough! In my experience they seem to go from almost done, almost done, almost done to burnt! I've also read, "The nuts toast until they tempt your nose," but all I can say is watch them, set a timer and don't walk away!

51

Caesar Salad

This may be the single most requested recipe that we have. When we make it for the catering company we prepare it by the gallons so I have modified this to be made in a food processor or blender. This recipe will make more dressing than you'll need; the dressing must be kept refrigerated because of the raw eggs, but it will keep refrigerated for up to 1 week.

FOR THE CAESAR DRESSING:
1 egg plus 2 egg yolks

1/4 cup fresh garlic, peeled and chopped

1 tablespoon anchovy paste or to taste

3 cups mild olive oil or olive oil/canola oil blend

1/2 teaspoon ground black pepper

1/2 cup Parmesan cheese, grated

1/2 cup lemon juice

FOR THE SALAD:
1 pound chopped hearts of Romaine

1-1/2 cups croutons, homemade (page 162) or store bought

3/4 cup Caesar Dressing, or to taste

1-2 tablespoons fresh grated Parmesan cheese

1. Place the egg and egg yolks, garlic, and anchovy paste in the work bowl of the food processor or blender. Blend ingredients and slowly add the olive oil to make a mayonnaise. Gradually fold in black pepper, Parmesan cheese and lemon juice by pulsing the machine, scraping down the sides of the bowl to mix well.

2. Toss all ingredients together.
Serves 8-10

HELPFUL HINT:This is a temperamental recipe. It can "break" very easily. Try to add the oil very slowly when making the mayonnaise base to avoid a curdled appearance.

NOTE: Raw egg preparations are generally considered safe for healthy adults, when handled with care. See page 171 for safe egg handling practices.

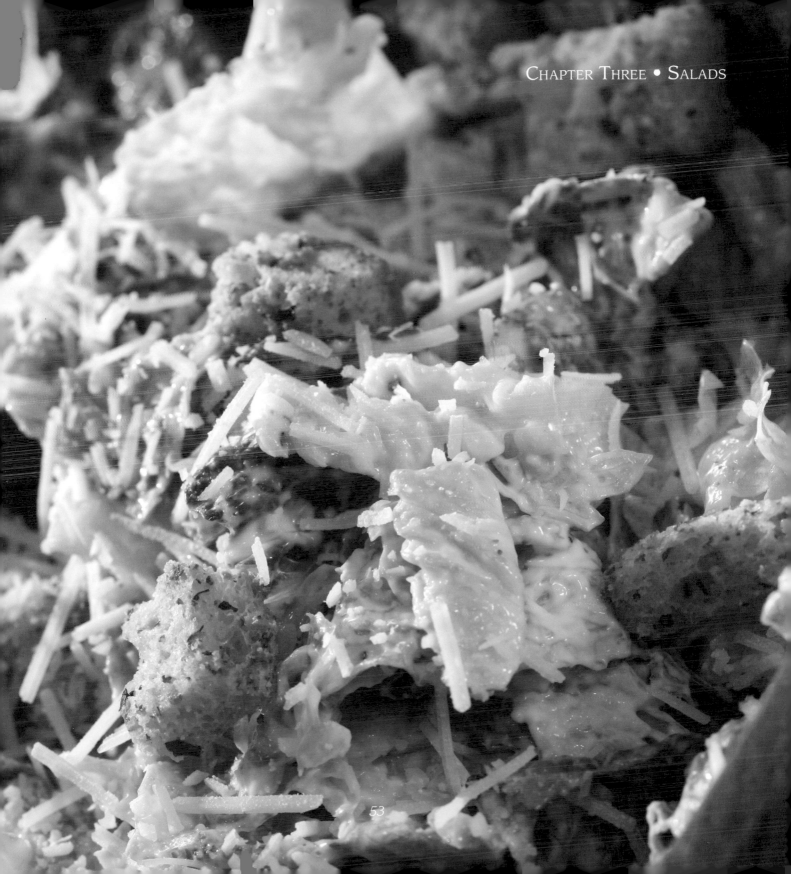

Asian Slaw with Cashews

This is a very tasty and simple recipe to go with summer evening barbecues. It can complement everything from seafood to steaks.

FOR SLAW:

1/4 pound snow peas (about 30 peas), strings removed

2 cups Napa cabbage, cut in thin shreds

2 cups red cabbage, cut in thin shreds

1 red and 1 yellow bell pepper, cored, seeded, cut in thin strips

4 green onions, sliced thin on the diagonal

1 carrot, peeled and grated

3/4 cup whole cashews, roasted and salted

FOR DRESSING:

1 small shallot, peeled and chopped

2 teaspoons Dijon mustard

2 tablespoons seasoned rice wine vinegar

2 tablespoons lemon juice

2 teaspoons soy sauce

1/4 teaspoon ground ginger

1/4 cup olive oil

1/4 cup corn oil

2 tablespoons sesame oil

1. Bring one quart of water to a boil in a saucepan. Add snow peas and blanch for 20 seconds. Drain and refresh under cold water. Cut snow peas into thin strips across the diagonal.

2. In a medium bowl add Napa cabbage, red cabbage, bell peppers, green onion, grated carrot, snow peas and cashews.

3. For the dressing combine shallot, Dijon, vinegar, lemon juice, soy sauce and ginger in the food processor or blender. With the motor running slowly, add the olive oil, corn oil and sesame oil.

4. Toss the salad with the dressing and serve.
   Serves 6-8

Wednesday Salad with Tarragon Vinaigrette

For lack of a better name, "Wednesday Salad" was served every Wednesday in our café. It remains a popular choice on our catering menu and is another one of those simple salads with very few ingredients that all work well together. I enjoy using this vinaigrette with the Chicken Salad (page 51), stuffed in a tomato.

FOR THE TARRAGON VINAIGRETTE:

2 shallots

1/2 ounce fresh tarragon leaves (about 1/2 cup)

2 tablespoons Dijon mustard

1 teaspoon salt

3/4 cup red wine vinegar

1/4 cup seasoned rice wine vinegar

2-3/4 cups olive oil

FOR THE SALAD:

10 ounces chopped romaine

10 ounces baby spinach

1 cup bacon, cooked, drained, chopped

1 cup toasted sliced almonds

3/4 cup crumbled feta cheese

3/4-1 cup Tarragon Vinaigrette

1. Add shallots to the work bowl of your food processor or blender and chop. Add tarragon, Dijon, salt, red wine vinegar and rice wine vinegar and blend. Slowly add olive oil and let blend until emulsified (thick and smooth).

2. In a salad bowl add romaine, baby spinach, bacon, almonds and feta. Toss with dressing and serve.
   Serves 8-10

HELPFUL HINT: I like to substitute butter lettuce for the romaine. It's a little more elegant and matches well with the dressing.

Cahoots House Salad with Balsamic Vinaigrette

This is a simple salad with very few ingredients. It's the combination of flavors that make it work so well. The recipe uses a homemade mayonnaise base similar to the Caesar dressing. If you have a problem with the raw eggs, you can also substitute store-bought mayonnaise (about 3 cups). As with the Caesar recipe, you'll have leftover dressing; be sure to keep it refrigerated.

FOR THE BALSAMIC VINAIGRETTE:
4 egg yolks

1 tablespoon garlic, chopped

2-1/2 cups mild olive oil

1/3 cup Dijon mustard

1-1/2 tablespoons lemon juice

1/2 cup balsamic vinegar

1/4 teaspoon black pepper

FOR THE SALAD:
8 ounces mixed baby greens

1/2 cup Balsamic Vinaigrette

1/2 cup Gorgonzola cheese, crumbled

1 cup croutons, preferably homemade
(recipe page 162)

1. Add egg yolks and garlic to the work bowl of your food processor or blender. Blend mixture as you slowly add the oil to make a mayonnaise.

2. Put the homemade mayonnaise in a separate bowl and carefully whisk in the mustard, lemon juice, balsamic vinegar, and black pepper.

3. Toss greens with dressing and top with cheese and croutons.
Serves 8-10

NOTE: Raw egg preparations are generally considered safe for healthy adults, when handled with care. See page 171 for safe egg handling practices.

Blue Cheese Wedge

Even though I am not a big fan of iceberg lettuce, this works for me and is actually one of my favorite salads. It's even making a bit of a comeback from the old steakhouse days and has found its way back on many trendy, new menus.

FOR THE BLUE CHEESE DRESSING:

1 cup mayonnaise

1/2 cup sour cream

1/4 cup buttermilk

2 cloves garlic, minced

1/4 cup fresh parsley, chopped

1 tablespoon lemon juice

1 tablespoon white balsamic vinegar

1-1/2 cups blue cheese, crumbled

1 teaspoon celery seed

1 teaspoon salt

1 teaspoon ground black pepper

FOR THE SALAD:

3 heads iceberg lettuce

2 cups Blue Cheese Dressing

1 cup cooked, chopped bacon

1 cup tomato, chopped

1/2 cup red onion chopped

Chopped fresh parsley

Fresh ground black pepper

1. Mix all the dressing ingredients together until well blended.

2. Wash and core the iceberg lettuce. Cut each head of lettuce in half and then in half again for a total of 12 wedges. Arrange 2 chunks of lettuce onto 6 plates.

3. Pour 1/3 to 1/2 cup of the blue cheese dressing over the lettuce wedges on each plate. Divide the bacon between the 6 plates and sprinkle over the blue cheese dressing. Top each salad with chopped tomato and chopped red onion. Garnish with chopped parsley and fresh ground pepper.
Serves 6

WINE SUGGESTION:
*This is a popular side dish to
a grilled steak and the blue
cheese and black pepper
in it make it a good match
with wines such as Merlot or
Cabernet Sauvignon*

59

Holiday Salad

We designed this salad to complement our winemaker dinners. This salad is very festive (hence the name). It is often difficult to pair wine with salad as most salad dressings contain vinegar, an ingredient that can argue with the wine. However, this dressing is made with pomegranate juice instead of vinegar, so it works well with light fruity reds. Again, you'll end up with more dressing than you'll need for the salad.

FOR THE POMEGRANATE DRESSING:

1 small shallot
(or half of 1 large shallot)

1 tablespoon Dijon mustard

1/2 teaspoon salt

1/2 cup pomegranate juice

1 cup mild olive oil

FOR THE SALAD:

8 ounces sweet baby lettuce greens (no radicchio or frisée)

1/2 cup chopped Maytag blue cheese or other Roquefort-style blue cheese

1/2 cup toasted walnuts

1/2 cup dried cranberries

1/2 cup Pomegranate Dressing

1. In the work bowl of the food processor or blender chop shallot. Add Dijon, salt and pomegranate juice. Blend while slowly adding the oil until thick and smooth.

2. Divide lettuce onto 6 to 8 salad plates or bowls. Evenly distribute and top the lettuce with the blue cheese, walnuts and dried cranberries. Drizzle each salad with 2 to 3 tablespoons of pomegranate dressing.
Serves 6-8

WINE SUGGESTION:
Syrah or Pinot Noir

61

CHAPTER FOUR

QUICHE & EGG DISHES

Soufflé Style Spinach Quiche

I adapted this recipe in the late 1970s when I was working for The Perfect Pan in San Diego. The first Cuisinart food processor had just been introduced and we were always looking for ideas to demonstrate the Cuisinart. I find this recipe to be the best of both worlds of soufflé and quiche: light and fluffy yet rich and creamy. If you would like to reduce the calories in this dish, you can substitute low fat or light cheeses and reduce the egg yolks to three.

10-inch deep dish pastry shell, store bought, homemade or other crust options (see page 154).

2 tablespoons unsalted butter

1/4 cup green onions, chopped

1 pound (16 ounces) frozen chopped spinach, thawed and drained

2 teaspoons Dijon mustard

1 teaspoon salt

1 teaspoon pepper

1/4 teaspoon ground nutmeg

1/2 pound jack cheese, softened, cut into 1-inch cubes

1/2 pound cream cheese, softened, cut into 1-inch cubes

5 eggs, separated

1. Preheat oven to 350 degrees F (325 convection).

2. Line the pastry crust with parchment paper and fill with dry beans, rice or pie weights. Bake for 8 minutes. Let cool and remove the weights and parchment.

3. Melt butter in a 12-inch skillet over medium heat. Add chopped green onions to the melted butter, sauté for about 2 minutes, stirring until soft.

4. Squeeze any excess water from the thawed spinach. Add spinach to butter mixture; continue cooking for an additional 2 minutes. Stir in Dijon, salt, pepper and nutmeg. Remove from heat and let cool slightly.

5. Put the jack cheese cubes and cream cheese cubes in the bowl of a food processor and pulse until smooth. Slowly add the 5 egg yolks one at a time, scraping down the side of the food processor bowl until mixture is incorporated.

6. Add the cooled spinach mixture into the food processor with the cheese and egg yolk mixture and pulse the machine, scraping down the sides of the processor bowl until blended.

7. In a separate bowl, whip the 5 egg whites until stiff.

8. In separate bowl, carefully fold the whipped egg whites into the spinach mixture. Spoon into prepared crust.

9. Bake for 30 to 40 minutes at 350 degrees F until the batter is puffed, set and golden. It is normal for it to fall a little when it comes out of the oven.
   Serves 8-10

HELPFUL HINT: Allow time for your cheeses to soften. You can put the cheese cubes in the microwave on medium low for 3 to 4 minutes to expedite this step. Be sure and try different crust options with this recipe. I like the Wild Rice Crust (see page 68).

Italian Sausage, Leek & Artichoke Quiche

We served this quiche in the restaurant and continue to include it in our catering business. It has become a popular choice for several of our local bed and breakfasts that purchase it to serve to their guests. I would keep it our little secret except they tell me that it is the most often requested recipe so the jig is up!

9-inch or 10-inch deep dish pastry shell, store bought, homemade or other crust options (see page 152).

4 tablespoons butter

1 cup leeks (2-3 leeks), thinly sliced and washed

1/2 pound hot Italian sausage, casings removed, cooked, drained and chopped

2, 6-ounce jars marinated artichoke hearts, well drained and chopped

4 eggs, slightly beaten

1 cup whipping cream

1 teaspoon salt

1/2 teaspoon pepper

1 teaspoon dry mustard powder

dash of hot sauce

1 teaspoon Italian seasoning

1/4 pound grated Swiss cheese (reserve 1/2 cup for top)

paprika

1. Preheat oven to 350 degrees F (325 convection).

2. Line the pastry crust with parchment paper and fill with dry beans, rice or pie weights. Bake for 8 minutes. Let cool and remove the weights and parchment.

3. Melt the butter over medium heat in a 12-inch skillet. Add sliced leeks and cook, stirring for about 3 minutes until soft and starting to brown.

4. Add cooked sausage, warm through. Add chopped artichoke, stir well and remove from heat to cool.

5. In a bowl, whisk together eggs, cream, salt, pepper, mustard powder, hot sauce and Italian seasoning.

6. Add all but 1/2 cup of the grated Swiss cheese to the prepared crust.

7. Gently pour the well-mixed egg custard mix over the cheese and quiche filling. Top with remaining 1/2 cup cheese. Sprinkle with paprika.

8. Bake for 30 to 40 minutes until filling is puffed, set and golden. Let rest for about 5 minutes before cutting.
   Serves 6-8

HELPFUL HINTS: Cleaning leeks can be a project. I like to slice them and then wash them.

When mixing the quiche custard, be sure the spices are well incorporated so they end up in the quiche and not at the bottom of the mixing bowl.

WINE SUGGESTION:
A light-bodied Zinfandel

Zucchini, Leek & Goat Cheese Quiche

We have successfully served this quiche at the annual Paso Robles Wine Festival for the past 15 years. We thought about trying something different from year to year but as the old saying goes "If it ain't broke don't fix it!" We estimate that over the years we have served over 11,000 portions, so I guess it's fair to say it's a crowd pleaser.

FOR THE WILD RICE CRUST:

2 cups vegetable or chicken stock

1 cup wild rice, uncooked

2 tablespoons unsalted butter, cut into pieces

1 egg, slightly beaten

1/4 cup Parmesan cheese, grated

2 tablespoons lemon

1. Preheat oven to 350 degrees F (325 convection)

2. Bring stock to a boil in a small sauce pan. Add the wild rice, bring back to a boil, reduce heat to medium low and simmer, covered until the rice is tender and the liquid is absorbed, about 1 hour.

3. Transfer cooked rice to a bowl, add the butter pieces, stir until melted and cool slightly.

4. When rice is cool enough to handle add egg, Parmesan cheese, and lemon juice. Mix well.

5. Press the rice mixture into a 9-inch or 10-inch deep dish pie pan, letting it come up the side of the pan in an even thickness. Bake at 350 degrees for 8-10 minutes until it begins to brown. Remove from oven and set aside.

continued on page 70...

HELPFUL HINT: Allow time for the zucchini to expel the extra moisture. Don't be afraid of over salting the squash; as the moisture is released the salt will dissipate (after 30 minutes). I also find it easier to wash the leeks after they have been sliced.

Zucchini, Leek & Goat Cheese Quiche

...continued from page 68

FOR THE QUICHE:
1-1/2 cups zucchini, grated

4 tablespoons unsalted butter

1-1/2 cups leeks, (about 2-3 leeks) thinly sliced and washed

4 eggs, lightly beaten

1 cup whipping cream

1 teaspoon Dijon mustard

1 teaspoon salt

1 teaspoon black pepper

1/2 teaspoon dried oregano leaf

1/2 teaspoon dried thyme leaf

1/4 teaspoon ground nutmeg

dash of hot sauce

1 cup grated Swiss cheese

4 ounces goat cheese, crumbled

1. Salt the grated zucchini, mix well and let it drain in a colander for about 30 minutes.

2. Preheat oven to 350 degrees F.

3. Melt butter over medium heat in a 12-inch skillet. Add sliced leeks and sauté until soft, about 2-3 minutes.

4. While the leeks are cooking squeeze all the liquid out of the zucchini in a few small batches. Add the zucchini to the leeks and continue cooking, stirring to mix well, for about 3-4 minutes more. Remove from heat to cool.

5. In a bowl combine eggs, cream, Dijon, salt, pepper, oregano, thyme, nutmeg and hot sauce. Mix well to distribute seasonings.

6. Add 3/4 cup of Swiss cheese to the top of the crust. Spread the zucchini leek filling over Swiss cheese. Crumble the goat cheese over the zucchini leek filling. Sprinkle the top of the filling with remaining 1/4 cup Swiss cheese. Pour egg custard over the top. Use a fork to help fluff and evenly distribute ingredients.

7. Bake 35-40 minutes until puffed, set and golden.
Serves 6-8

Grilled Chicken Chili Relleno Quiche

Technically this is not a chili relleno at all, but we call it that because it contains some of the ingredients that are often found in that dish. We like to start with a tortilla crust and fill it with a mixture of jack and cheddar cheeses, diced green chilies, shredded grilled chicken and sautéed vegetables, all in a spiced egg mixture.

4 large flour tortillas, preferably chipotle flavored

1 pound jack & cheddar cheese blend (or 1/2 pound each), grated

2 tablespoons butter

1/2 cup red onion, chopped

1/2 cup red bell pepper, chopped

1/2 cup cut corn

8 mild green chilies, chopped and drained well

1/2 pound (about 2 cups) grilled chicken breast, shredded

12 eggs

4 cups half & half

1 tablespoon salt

1/2 tablespoon pepper

1 teaspoon cumin

1/2 teaspoon oregano

2 dashes of hot sauce

1. Preheat oven to 350 degrees F.

2. Lightly butter the bottom of a 13x9x2-inch baking pan. Line the baking dish with the tortillas, carefully over lapping them to cover the bottom and sides. Spread 3/4 of the cheese over the tortilla crust.

3. Melt butter in a skillet. Add chopped onion and cook until soft, about 2 minutes. Add bell pepper, cut corn, green chilies and chicken. Continue cooking another 2-3 minutes until warmed through. Set aside to cool slightly.

4. In a separate mixing bowl whip eggs until well mixed. Add half & half, salt, pepper, cumin, oregano, and hot sauce. Mix well.

5. Top the crust and cheese mixture with the sautéed vegetable and chicken and spread evenly. Top with remaining cheese. Pour the egg mixture over the top.

6. Bake at 350 degrees F for 30-40 minutes
   Serves 10-12

HELPFUL HINT; If you warm the tortillas slightly they will be more pliable and easier to work with.

Ham & Asparagus Strata

"Strata" comes from the word "stratum," a geological term meaning horizontal layers, one upon another. How it navigated its way into the kitchen I'm not sure, but it does make for great layers of flavor.

1 pound asparagus (about 1 bunch), cut into 1/2-inch pieces

8 cups (packed) 1-inch bread cubes, about 14 slices.

2-1/4 cups milk

5 large eggs

1-1/2 cups whipping cream

1-1/2 teaspoons salt

1/2 teaspoon pepper

1/4 teaspoon nutmeg

1 tablespoon Dijon mustard

1 pound ham, diced (about 4 cups)

3 cups Swiss cheese, grated

paprika

1. Preheat oven to 350 degrees F (325 convection). Butter a 13x9x2-inch baking dish.

2. Blanch asparagus pieces in salted boiling water until they turn bright green, approximately 2 minutes. To stop cooking process, immediately place asparagus in bowl of ice water. Drain well before using.

3. Combine bread and milk in a bowl and let sit for about 15 minutes.

4. In a separate bowl, whisk eggs until blended, add cream, salt, pepper, nutmeg and Dijon, whisk until blended.

5. Place half the bread mixture in prepared baking dish. Top with half the asparagus, half the ham and half the cheese. Repeat layers with remaining bread, asparagus, ham and cheese.

6. Pour the cream mixture over the top. Sprinkle with paprika. Bake at 350 degrees F uncovered until set in the middle, about an hour.
Serves 10-12

HELPFUL HINT: You can use any bread you like; white, wheat, sourdough, focaccia, brioche, all will bring a different taste and texture to the dish.

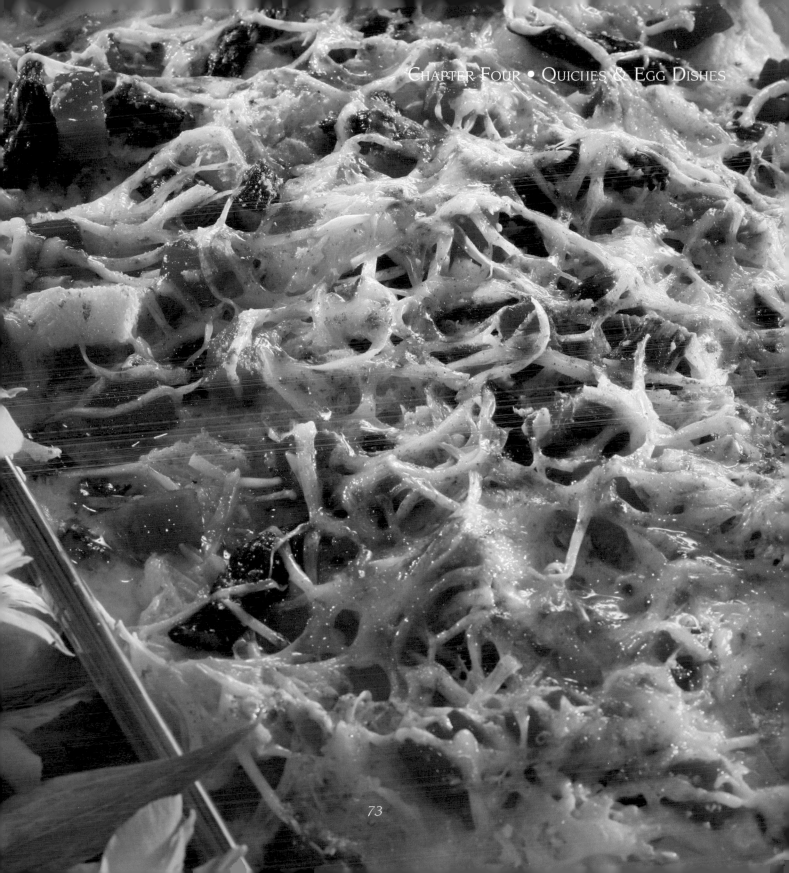

Lisa's Leftover Thanksgiving Strata

Our local newspaper approached me about a recipe for leftover Thanksgiving turkey. I was certain there was no room for another turkey Tetrazzini recipe, so I came up with this dish, which can be prepared the night before (actually as you put away dinner), refrigerated and baked the next morning. The key to this dish is the dressing/stuffing. Feel free to try it using dressing made with sausage, nuts or fruits, and try a different cheese or combination of cheeses to suit your taste; I like white cheddar sage.

8 cups leftover dressing

3/4-pound (about 3 cups) cooked diced turkey

2 cups shredded Monterey Jack cheese

2/3 cup whole berry cranberry sauce

8 eggs

3 cups half & half

1 teaspoon each salt & pepper or to taste

1. Preheat oven to 350 degrees F. Butter a 13x9x2-inch glass baking dish.

2. Place half the dressing in a single layer in prepared baking dish (dressing may not cover bottom of baking dish).

3. Top with half of the turkey, 1/3 cup cranberry sauce and 1 cup cheese. Repeat layering with remaining dressing, turkey, cranberry sauce and cheese.

4. In separate bowl, whisk eggs, half & half and seasonings. Pour over top of the strata. Bake uncovered at 350 degrees F until firm in the center, puffed and golden, about 50-60 minutes.
Serves 10-12

Wild Mushroom Forestière

"Forestière" is a French term meaning "of the forest," referring to the wild mushrooms in this recipe. You may use regular mushrooms if you don't care for the wild mushroom flavors. This is an excellent choice for a special occasion brunch as it is very delicious and unusual and can be prepared ahead of time through step 5 and refrigerated overnight.

FOR WILD MUSHROOM FILLING:

4 tablespoons butter

4 tablespoons olive oil

4 cups finely minced assorted mushrooms, such as cremini, shiitake, oyster, chanterelle or portabello

1/4 cup minced shallots

1/4 cup flour

1 cup cream

1/4 teaspoon salt

1/4 teaspoon pepper

1. Preheat oven to 400 degrees F (375 convection).

2. Butter a 13x9x2-inch baking dish.

3. For the mushroom filling, heat 4 tablespoons butter and olive oil in a sauté pan over moderate heat. Add mushrooms and shallots and stir frequently for about 5 minutes. Lower heat and sprinkle with 1/4 cup flour, mix well, add cream and stir until thickened, about 1 minute. Season with salt and pepper. Set aside.

continued on page 76...

Wild Mushroom Forestière

...*continued from page 75*

FOR EGG MIXTURE:

1 cup flour

4 cups milk

1/2 cup butter, cut into pieces

1 teaspoon salt

1/4 teaspoon pepper

1/8 teaspoon nutmeg

3 cups Swiss cheese (you may use Jarlsberg, Gruyere, Emmenthaler or any combination that suits your taste)

8 eggs

4. For the egg mixture, put 1 cup of flour and milk in a sauce pan over medium high heat, whisking slowly until it comes to a boil. Remove from heat. Whisk in butter pieces, salt, pepper, nutmeg, 2-1/4 cups Swiss cheese, 3/4 cup Swiss cheese, add the eggs one at a time. Mix well.

5. Pour half of the egg mixture into the bottom of the prepared baking dish. Spoon mushroom mixture over the egg mixture, then cover with remaining egg mixture and top with remaining 3/4 cup Swiss cheese.

6. Bake at 400 degrees F for about 30 minutes (40 minutes if it has been refrigerated).
Serves 10-12

WINE SUGGESTION:
A hearty red such as a Pinot Noir, Syrah or Mourvèdre

Southwestern Frittata with Chorizo

My family owned a restaurant in Goleta, California in the early 1980s, and we served quite a variety of frittatas on our menu. They work well for any meal, any time of day. Serve this with salsa, guacamole and sour cream.

12 large eggs

salt and pepper to taste

1 tablespoon unsalted butter

1 cup red onion, chopped

1/2 cup red bell pepper, chopped

1/2 cup corn kernels (about 1 ear of fresh corn) or frozen, thawed

1/4 cup sliced, drained pickled jalapeño chilies

4, 6-inch corn tortillas, cut in 1/2-inch strips

12 ounces chorizo, casings removed, cooked and drained

1/4 cup cilantro, chopped

1 cup grated cheddar/jack cheese blend

1. Preheat broiler.

2. Beat eggs in a medium bowl, season with salt and pepper.

3. Melt butter in a 12-inch non-stick oven proof skillet. Add onion, bell pepper, corn, sliced jalapeños and tortilla strips and continue to cook for another 2 to 3 minutes stirring occaisionally until well combined.

4. Add egg mixture, cooked chorizo and cilantro to the skillet and stir to blend. Top with grated cheese.

5. Cover skillet, reduce heat to low and cook frittata until just about set, approximately 5 minutes.

6. Uncover skillet. Broil frittata until top is set, puffed and starting to brown, about 2 minutes. Cut into wedges and either serve out of the pan or place wedges on individual plates.
Serves 6-8

WINE SUGGESTION:
Tempranillo or Zinfandel

PASTA, RICE & BEANS

Grown-up Macaroni & Cheese

Through the years in the restaurant and catering company this has come to be known as "Gourmet Macaroni and Cheese," but our niece Ellie and nephew Brian, ages 5 and 7, gobble this right up. The recipe is rarely ever the same, but it's always delicious and loaded with cheese. You can use any combination of cheeses including smoked cheeses.

1/4 pound unsalted butter

1/2 cup garlic, chopped

1/2 cup flour

5 cups whole milk, warmed

1/2 pound goat cheese

1 tablespoon salt

2 teaspoons ground black pepper

1/2 teaspoon ground nutmeg

2 pounds macaroni (see note)*

4 quarts water

1 tablespoon salt

1/4 cup olive oil

1/2 pound Swiss cheese, grated

1/2 pound blue cheese, crumbled

1/2 pound sharp cheddar, grated

1/2 pound Fontina, grated

1/2 cup shredded Parmesan (reserved for topping)

1. Preheat oven to 350 degrees F.

2. Melt butter in a 4-quart sauce pan over medium-low heat. Add garlic and cook slowly, stirring often until soft, about 5 minutes.

3. Add flour and continue cooking, stirring often for about 5 more minutes. Add milk and continue cooking until the milk reaches the consistency of heavy cream.

4. Crumble in goat cheese and stir until dissolved. Add salt, pepper, and nutmeg. Remove from heat and set aside.

5. To make pasta, bring 4 quarts of water, 1 tablespoon of salt and 1/4 cup of olive oil to a boil. Add pasta and cook until al dente, about 10 minutes depending on the type of macaroni you use. Drain and put pasta in a large mixing bowl.

6. Pour the thickened goat cheese/milk mixture over the pasta and stir. Add the rest of the grated cheeses and mix well.

7. Butter a 13x9x2-inch baking dish or other 3-quart casserole dish. Spoon the pasta cheese mixture into the prepared pan. Top with Parmesan and bake at 350 degrees F for 25-30 minutes or until top is starting to brown and bubble. You may want to place the baking dish on a sheet pan in case it bubbles over.

Serves 12

*NOTE: Most macaroni are tube shaped pasta like elbow, ziti and penne. Other forms include shells and twists.

Fettuccini Alfredo

Roman restaurateur Alfredo di Lello is credited for creating this dish in the 1920s. Don't let the simplicity of this dish fool you. This is a good example of a recipe where great ingredients matter. Use a good quality fresh grated Parmesan like Reggiano Parmigiano, homemade or fresh pasta, and plentiful grindings of fresh ground pepper.

1/4 cup olive oil

2 teaspoons salt

1/4 pound butter

1-1/3 cup heavy cream

1 pound fettuccini noodles

1-1/4 cup freshly grated Parmesan cheese

1/4 teaspoon salt

fresh ground black pepper

chopped fresh parsley

1. Bring 4 quarts of water to a boil. Add 1/4 cup olive oil and 2 teaspoons of salt.

2. Melt butter in a 12-inch skillet over medium-high heat. When the butter is melted add cream. Cook mixture until it starts to thicken and bubble, add Parmesan and salt and remove from heat.

3. Cook fettuccini in boiling water until "al dente." Drain and toss into a warmed serving bowl. Pour sauce over pasta, toss well and top with fresh ground pepper and parsley.
   Serves 4 as a first course or 2 as an entrée

Wine suggestion:
Chardonnay, Chianti or
Nebbiolo

Warm Arugula Pesto Pasta

Olea Farms is one of many local olive oil farms on the California Central Coast. Clothilde and Yves Julien own and operate this beautiful farm in Templeton, and this recipe is a variation of one from their cookbook "Olea's Secret Recipes."

1 cup arugula, packed

1/2 cup basil leaves, packed

2 tablespoons lemon juice

2 cloves garlic, finely chopped

1/2 cup Parmesan, grated

1 cup Olea Farms Arbequina olive oil, or other extra virgin olive oil

salt and pepper

1 pound Penne pasta

2 chicken breasts, smoked or grilled

1 cup marinated feta and olives, (recipe page 160)

1-1/2 cups cherry tomatoes, cut in half

1. Place arugula, basil, lemon juice, garlic and Parmesan in the food processor or blender. With the machine running, add olive oil. Season with salt and pepper. Set aside.

2. Cook penne pasta in a large pot of salted boiling water for about 9 minutes or until "al dente." Drain pasta. Return pasta to the pot.

3. Slice warm chicken breast into 1/4-inch slices.

4. Add pesto to the drained pasta, after mixing well, spoon into serving dish. Top with marinated feta and olives, sliced chicken breast, and cherry tomatoes.
   Serves 4-6

NOTE: Arugula, a spicy winter green, flourishes year round. It literally grows wild in my garden. It is a healthy addition to salads, sandwiches and pasta dishes. Arugula is a cruciferous vegetable and contains the phytochemicals called indoles, thought to be cancer-fighters, as well as beta-carotene and more Vitamin C than any other salad green. It also supplies folate (folic acid) and some calcium.

Arroz Verde

Some of my favorite cooking memories come from the time I spent working for The Perfect Pan in Southern California as a cooking school assistant. One of my favorite teachers was Diana Kennedy, who has written several books on the regional cooking of Mexico. This recipe is an adaptation of a recipe she makes in her book "My Mexico."

4 jalapeños, seeded

4 tomatillos, husks peeled and rinsed

1, 10-ounce package frozen chopped spinach, thawed and drained

2 teaspoons salt

1-1/2 cups water

2 tablespoons vegetable oil

1-1/2 cups long grain white rice, rinsed well

1/2 cup white onion, finely chopped

4 cloves garlic, peeled and chopped

2 tablespoons fresh lime juice

1/4 cup cilantro leaves, roughly chopped

1. In a blender, puree the jalapeños, tomatillos, spinach and salt in 1/2 cup of water.

2. Heat oil in a sauce pan over medium-high heat. Add rice, cook until the rice begins to toast, about 5 minutes. Add onion and garlic and cook for a few more minutes. Add the chili puree and the remaining 1 cup of water. Reduce heat to low, cover and cook until the liquid is absorbed, about 15 minutes.

3. Just before the rice is finished, stir in lime juice and cilantro. Cook an additional 5 minutes.
   Serves 6

Coconut Ginger Rice

This is a great dish to jazz up a summer barbeque. I like to serve this rice with mixed grill kebobs and a green salad.

2 tablespoons vegetable oil

4 cloves garlic, chopped

2 tablespoons fresh ginger, peeled and chopped

1 Serrano chili, thinly sliced (optional)

2 cups uncooked long grain white rice, rinsed well

2 cups water

1 cup coconut milk

1 teaspoon salt

4 green onions, thinly sliced

2-3 tablespoons cilantro, stemmed and coarsely chopped

1. Heat oil in a sauce pan over medium-high heat. Add garlic, ginger and Serrano chili, stir quickly for about 1 minute.

2. Add rice, continue cooking, stirring for 2 more minutes. Add water, coconut milk, and salt and bring mixture to a boil. Reduce heat to low and simmer, covered, until rice is tender and the liquid is absorbed, about 25-30 minutes.

3. Remove from heat and stir in half of the green onions and cilantro.

4. Transfer rice to a serving dish and top with remaining green onions and cilantro.
Serves 4-6

Wild Mushroom, Blue Cheese & Walnut Risotto

Risotto is the ultimate comfort food for me, but I find some people are intimidated by this dish. It isn't really that challenging, just a bit labor intensive. Once you get the hang of it you will find yourself whipping up all sorts of combinations. You can stir in a little chopped cooked chicken breast at the end and have a one-pot meal. The possibilities are as endless as the satisfaction.

5 tablespoons butter

6 cups chicken stock (recipe page 157)

1 medium yellow onion, diced

1-1/2 cups Arborio rice

8 ounces wild mushrooms, preferably shiitake, sliced

4 ounces Maytag blue cheese, or other blue cheese, crumbled

1/2 cup walnuts, toasted and coarsely chopped

1/2 cup shredded Parmesan cheese

1/2 teaspoon fresh ground black pepper

1 tablespoon parsley, chopped for garnish

1. Melt 4 tablespoons of the butter in a medium saucepan.

2. In a second pot, heat chicken stock to a simmer.

3. Add onion to the saucepan with the melted butter and sauté until soft and translucent.

4. Add Arborio rice to the onion; stir to combine. Add 1/2 cup of warm chicken stock. Continue stirring. As the mixture begins to absorb the stock it will thicken and start to "sing" – actually more like a whistle. Continue adding stock, 1/2 cup at a time, stirring, until the stock is absorbed and the rice is tender or all the stock has been added. About 20 minutes.

5. In a separate pan melt remaining tablespoon of butter. Add sliced mushrooms and sauté for 1-2 minutes. Set aside.

6. Once the rice is tender and the stock is absorbed, add blue cheese, walnuts, mushrooms, and Parmesan cheese, stir to combine. Garnish with pepper and parsley and serve.
Serves 4-6

WINE SUGGESTION:
A hearty red such as a Petite Sirah, Mourvèdre or Zinfandel

Cahoots Black Beans

We've been making these black beans for the café and catering company from the beginning. We use them on our barbeque menu, in the black bean torte (page 21), and in our famous black bean, green chili and cheese burritos.

2 cups dried black beans

5 strips of uncooked bacon, sliced into 1/2-inch pieces

1 large red onion, peeled and chopped

4 cups chicken stock

1 teaspoon cumin

1 teaspoon dried oregano

2 teaspoons granulated garlic

1 teaspoon ground black pepper

2 teaspoons salt

1 teaspoon paprika

1/2 teaspoon crushed red pepper

1/4 teaspoon ground cloves

1. Cover beans with 4 cups water and soak overnight.

2. Cook bacon in a 4-quart stock pot until it begins to crisp.

3. Add chopped onion and cook until soft, about 5 minutes.

4. Drain the water off the black beans and add to the bacon and onion mixture along with chicken stock and the remaining herbs and spices.

5. Simmer uncovered for about 1 hour, until soft. You can serve these beans as is or you can partially mash them for a smoother texture.
Serves 6-8

Bourbon Baked Beans

I'm a little embarrassed to share this recipe because it is not made completely from scratch, however, it's easy, delicious and over the years has grown to be one of the most often requested barbeque side dishes that we do.

4 slices uncooked bacon, sliced into 1/2-inch pieces

4-6 cloves garlic

1 medium onion, chopped

1/4 cup molasses

1/4 cup yellow mustard

1/4 cup ketchup

1/4 cup bourbon

2 tablespoons brown sugar

2 tablespoons Worcestershire sauce

2, 28-ounce cans baked beans

1. Cook bacon in an 8-quart stock pot, over medium high heat until it begins to crisp.

2. Reduce heat to medium. Add chopped garlic and onion and cook until soft, be careful not to burn the garlic (about 3 to 4 minutes).

3. Add remaining ingredients and simmer over medium low heat for 30 minutes.
Serves 8-10

CHAPTER SIX

Vegetables & Sides

93

Broccoli with Wasabi Breadcrumbs & Pickled Ginger

Wasabi is a Japanese root, very similar to horseradish, with a strong fiery flavor. You can use either wasabi paste or hydrate wasabi powder with water to form the necessary amount of paste.

2 tablespoons olive oil

2 tablespoons unsalted butter

1 tablespoons wasabi paste

2 tablespoons soy sauce

1-1/2 cups coarse dry breadcrumbs

3 bunches (about 1-1/2 pounds) broccoli crowns, trimmed and cut into florets

1/2 cup pickled ginger

2 tablespoons sesame seeds, toasted

1. Melt olive oil and butter together in a large sauté pan.

2. Add wasabi paste and soy sauce and stir until combined. Add the breadcrumbs and sauté, stirring until golden brown and crisp. Set aside.

3. Bring water to a boil in a large stock pot fitted with a steam rack. Add broccoli and steam until crisp tender, about 3-5 minutes.

4. Transfer mixture to a serving dish and toss with wasabi bread crumbs and top with pickled ginger and sesame seeds.
Serves 6-8

Ratatouille

Ratatouille comes from the Provence region of France; it is a very versatile dish. It is fabulous on its own as a side dish or Bruschetta appetizer but I also like to incorporate it into frittatas, spoon it over grilled chicken or fish or serve it with spaghetti squash. This is a perfect dish to make in the summer when the garden is bursting at the seams with fresh vegetables, herbs and vine-ripe tomatoes.

1/2 cup extra virgin olive oil

1 large onion, coarsely chopped

1 heaping tablespoon garlic, chopped

2 bell peppers, preferably yellow and red, cut into 1/2-inch pieces

1 small eggplant, peeled and cut into 1/2-inch cubes

8 large tomatoes, peeled, seeded and chopped (or 2, 28-ounce cans of peeled diced tomatoes)

2 summer squash (zucchini, crookneck, patty pan or any combination), cut into 1/2-inch pieces

1/2 pound mushrooms, sliced

1/2 cup red wine

1/4 cup coarsely chopped fresh basil

2 teaspoons chopped fresh oregano

1 teaspoon chopped fresh rosemary

1 teaspoon chopped fresh thyme

1/2 teaspoon crushed red pepper

2 teaspoons salt or to taste

1 teaspoon fresh ground pepper

1. Heat olive oil in a large saucepan over medium heat. Add onion and garlic and cook for about 5 minutes or until soft.

2. Add the remaining vegetables, cook for an additional 3 to 4 minutes. Add red wine and herbs and spices. Cover and simmer for about 1 hour.
   Serves 4-6

HELPFUL HINT: To peel tomatoes, slip them into a pot of rapidly boiling water for 30 seconds. Remove and allow to cool. Peel off the blanched skins, then slice each tomato in half crosswise and gently squeeze to remove the seeds.

Wine suggestion:
Pinot Blanc or Nebbiolo

Roasted Baby Potatoes with Garlic & Herbs

I like to use baby Yukon gold, red, white, or purple potatoes, or a combination of colors for a very pretty presentation. A simple and delicious, yet understated and modest side dish that will match well with just about anything you serve.

1 pound baby potatoes (try to get them about the same size; you may need to cut the bigger potatoes in half.)

2 tablespoons olive oil

about 1/2 teaspoon each of salt and fresh ground pepper

3 cloves garlic, chopped

2 tablespoons mixed fresh herbs such as, parsley, thyme, rosemary, chives, or oregano.

1. Preheat oven to 450 degrees F.

2. Bring 4 quarts of water to a boil in a stockpot. Add the potatoes and boil for 8 minutes.

3. Drain potatoes and place on a baking sheet. Add olive oil and salt and pepper and toss well to coat.

4. Bake for 10 minutes at 450 degrees F. Remove from the oven and add garlic and herbs. Mix well. Return to the oven and bake for an additional 10 minutes until crispy and golden brown.
Serves 4-6

Asparagus with Meyer Lemon & Olive Oil

I love Meyer lemons. They seem to have a little more complexity to them than regular lemons and even have edible skins. Because of their apparent affinity for growing on the Central Coast of California, they have become identified as one of our signature citrus crops. This is a great summer recipe, especially when done on the grill with a grill basket. It can also be made with Pasolivo's Meyer Lemon olive oil.

2 bunches asparagus,
about 2 pounds

3 tablespoons extra virgin
olive oil

2 Meyer lemons, zested and
juiced

1 teaspoon kosher salt

1/2 teaspoon fresh ground
black pepper

1. Preheat oven to 425 F. Trim the stems of the asparagus and lay out onto a baking sheet. Toss with olive oil, lemon juice, salt and pepper.

2. Roast in the oven for about 10 minutes or until they are crisp tender. Remove from the oven and put into a serving dish. Sprinkle with lemon zest and serve.
Serves 6-8

Colorful Cauliflower Gratin

There are so many fun colors of cauliflower these days! I like to mix the white, green and orange, but if you can't find colorful cauliflower it also works with regular white cauliflower.

2 cups white cauliflower, cut into florets

2 cups orange cauliflower, cut into florets

2 cups green cauliflower, cut into florets

1/4 cup extra virgin olive oil

2 tablespoons lemon juice

1/4 cup shredded Parmesan cheese

1/2 cup smoked Fontina cheese, grated

1. Preheat oven to 350 degrees F.

2. Bring water to boil in a large stock pot fitted with a steamer rack and steam cauliflower until just crisp tender, about 3-5 minutes, though the actual time will depend on the size of the florets. Drain and put in a medium bowl.

3. Add olive oil, lemon juice and Parmesan and toss together. Transfer the cauliflower mixture to a gratin dish or baking dish. Top with grated smoked Fontina. Bake for 4-5 minutes and serve.
Serves 6-8

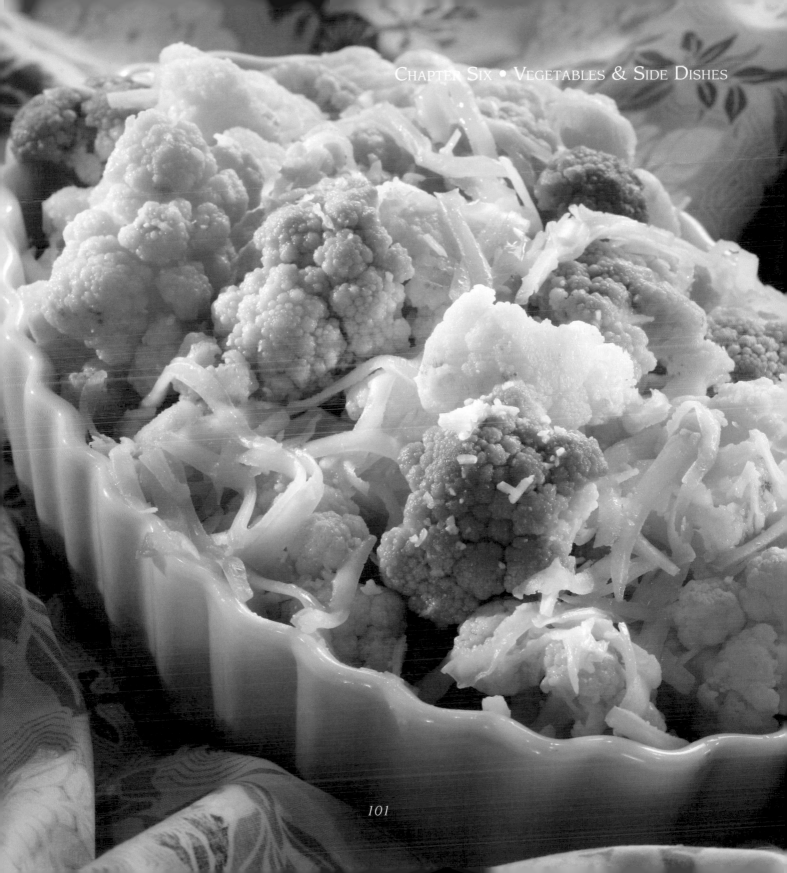

Twice Baked Potatoes

This was another favorite in the restaurant. We offered a "lite" version of this recipe as well but it did not sell as well as these – go figure!

5 russet potatoes, washed

1/2 cup sour cream

1/2 pound bacon, cooked, drained and crumbled

1/4 cup Parmesan cheese

1-1/2 cup cheddar/jack cheese blend, grated

1/2 cup red onion, diced

1 stick (1/4 pound) unsalted butter, cut in cubes

1/2 teaspoon salt

1/2 teaspoon fresh ground black pepper

1. Preheat oven to 400 degrees F.

2. Bake potatoes for about 60 minutes or until done. Let cool.

3. While potatoes are cooking, assemble the rest of the ingredients in a medium-size bowl.

4. When the potatoes are cool enough to handle but still warm, cut them in half lengthwise. With a large spoon scoop the potato flesh out of the shell of each half potato and add to the bowl. Mash the potato flesh with sour cream, bacon, Parmesan, 1/2 cup of the cheddar/jack blend, onion, salt and pepper and mix well.

5. Arrange the 10 potato shells cut side up on a cookie sheet. Divide the potato mixture evenly between each potato shell. Top with remaining 1 cup of cheddar/jack cheese. Sprinkle with paprika.

6. Reduce oven to 350 degrees F. and bake until warmed through, about 25-30 minutes or reheat in the microwave on medium-high heat for about 2-3 minutes.
Serves 8-10

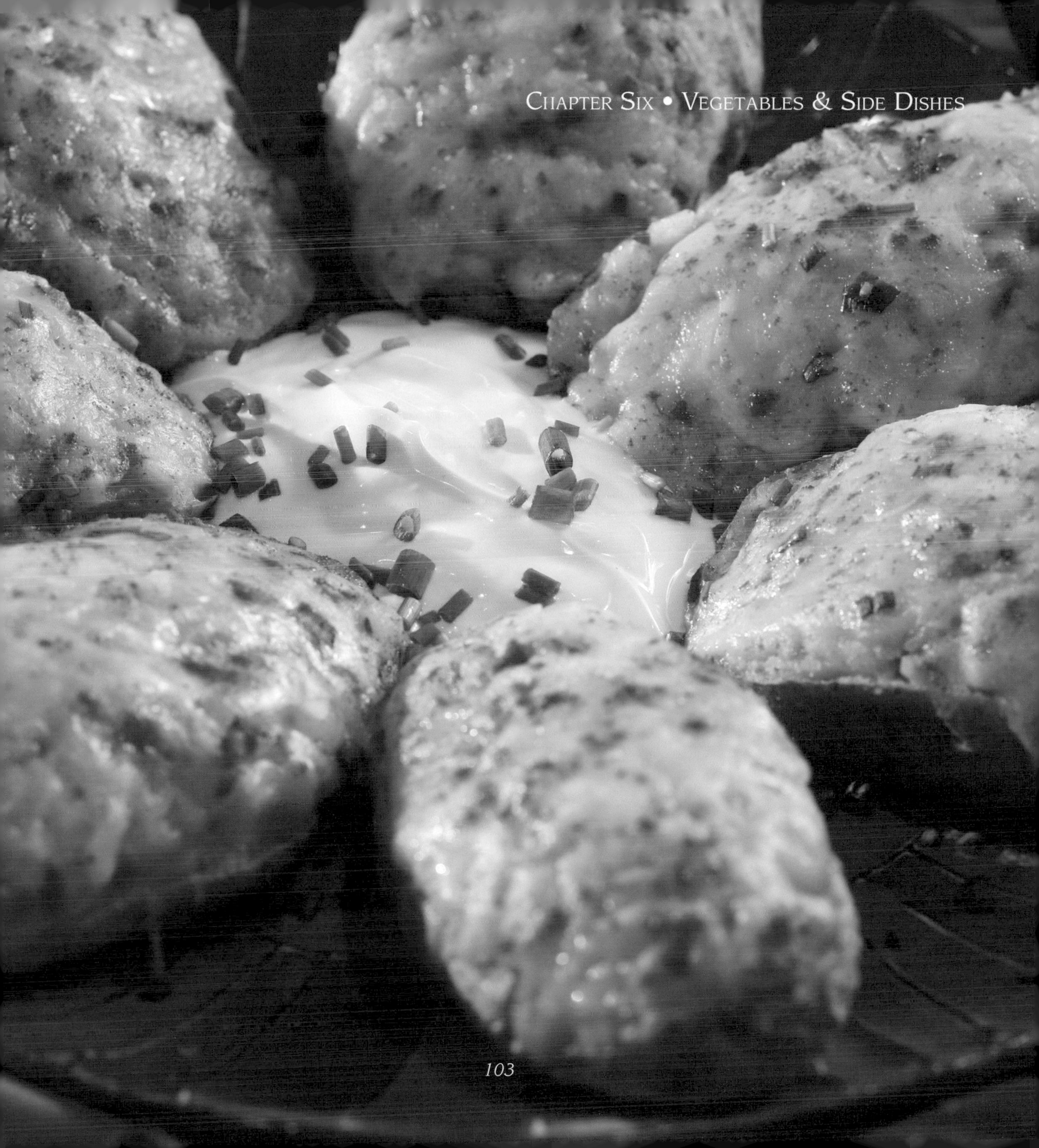

Scalloped Potatoes in Garlic & Cream

We get a lot of great feedback on this recipe, which is our take on delicious and decadent classic potatoes au gratin. It makes a wonderful side dish, and I also like to add wild mushrooms to give it even more texture and flavor.

3 pounds Yukon gold or russet potatoes, peeled, placed in a bowl and covered with cold water so they don't discolor

3-1/2 cups half & half

2 cups heavy cream

4 cloves garlic, chopped

2 teaspoons salt

1/2 teaspoon white pepper

1/4 teaspoon ground nutmeg

8 ounces Swiss cheese, grated

paprika

1. Preheat oven to 350 degrees F. Butter a 13x9x2-inch baking dish.

2. Combine half & half and cream in a saucepan.

3. Prepare your food processor with the 1/4-inch slicing blade. Carefully load the peeled potatoes into the feed tube and slice horizontally with consistent pressure. Add slices to the cream mixture. Be sure to include any of the potato juice that is expelled during slicing; it is full of starch and will help the thickening process.

4. Heat cream mixture in sauce pan over medium-low heat. Add garlic, salt, white pepper and nutmeg. Warm slowly, stirring frequently, until the mixture is thick and bubbly, about 20 minutes.

5. Pour mixture into baking dish. Top with grated Swiss cheese, sprinkle with paprika. Bake at 350 degrees F. for 30 minutes or until brown and bubbly.
Serves 10-12

HELPFUL HINT: Try adding 1 pound sautéed wild mushrooms to the potatoes or you can try substituting a different cheese.

Garlic Mashed Potatoes

Yes, more garlic! I suppose by now you have figured out that this edible bulb finds it way into many of our dishes. When we had the restaurant we kept a large bowl of mints on the counter to help with the residual garlic breath, but remember it's so good for you (and hopefully your family and friends). The trick to these potatoes is to boil the garlic with the potatoes to tone down the pungency.

2 pounds red potatoes

1/3 cup garlic cloves, peeled

6 tablespoons butter, melted

3/4 cup half and half, warmed

1 tablespoon salt

1 teaspoon ground white pepper

1. Put the red potatoes and garlic in a medium saucepan. Cover with water and bring to a boil over high heat.

2. Cook potatoes until tender. Drain in a colander and let sit for about 2 minutes.

3. Place cooked potatoes and garlic in a mixing bowl. Add butter, half and half, salt and pepper and mash with a potato masher. Using a hand held mixer or stand mixer whip the potatoes until fluffy and smooth, about 1 minute.

4. Place potatoes in a serving dish, cover and keep warm until ready to serve.
Serves 4-6

Roasted Brussels Sprouts with Macadamia Gremolata

Traditionally, "gremolata" is a garnish made from parsley, lemon zest and garlic and is most commonly served over Osso Buco. I find it works well as a garnish over all kinds of meats and vegetables. As a twist, I like adding nuts for a little crunch and texture.

2 pound Brussels sprouts, ends trimmed and cut in half

1/4 cup, plus 2 tablespoons extra virgin olive oil

Kosher salt and fresh ground pepper

1 cup macadamia nuts, roasted and salted, coarsely chopped

1/2 cup fresh parsley, finely chopped

Zest and juice from 2 lemons

2 cloves garlic, minced

1. Preheat oven to 375 degrees F.

2. Toss the Brussels sprouts with 1/4 cup olive oil and arrange on a baking sheet. Sprinkle with salt and pepper. Roast in the oven stirring occasionally, until the Brussels sprouts are tender, about 20 minutes.

3. In a separate bowl, mix together the remaining 2 tablespoons olive oil, macadamia nuts, parsley, lemon juice, zest and garlic.

4. When the Brussels sprouts are done, transfer them to a serving dish and top with gremolata.
Serves 6-8

CHAPTER SEVEN

Entrées

Prime Rib

"Prime Rib" is actually a reference to the quality and grade of the meat, in this case a whole rib eye. We use choice or better on all occasions, with "prime" being the highest USDA beef grade. Proper seasoning and slow roasting is key to a perfect prime rib roast. You can usually find choice or better at your big box stores or local butcher.

6-8 pound boneless rib eye

1/2 cup Cahoots House Rub or your favorite all purpose seasoning

Store-bought or homemade horseradish sauce as garnish

1. Preheat oven to 425 degrees F.

2. Place the roast in a roasting pan, fat side up, and generously rub seasoning over the entire roast. Bake for 30 minutes at 425 degrees F.

3. Reduce heat to 300 degrees F and continue cooking for 2 hours. At this time begin testing for doneness. Insert an instant read thermometer into the thickest part of the roast, it should read 135 degrees F for rare, 140 for medium rare. Once the roast reaches the desired temperature remove from oven and let the roast rest for 10-15 minutes; the internal temperature will continue to rise another 5-8 degrees.

4. Transfer to a serving platter. Serve with creamy or straight horseradish.
Serves 8-10

HELPFUL HINT: Putting your meat out (covered) on the counter for about 30 minutes before cooking and bringing it to room temperature (about 70 degrees F), will allow the meat to cook more evenly and consistently.

WINE SUGGESTION:
Syrah, Petite Sirah or Cabernet
Sauvignon

Italian Sausage Lasagna

I would have to say that over the years our lasagnas have been the flagships of our business. We have served a variety of flavors including, Veggie, Mediterranean, Mushroom Lovers, Southwestern Chicken and Cajun. This Italian sausage version is by far the most popular. This recipe will give you our basic formula, then you can concoct your own creations.

1 pound ricotta cheese

1/4 cup grated Parmesan cheese

12 ounces frozen chopped spinach, thawed and drained well; squeeze out all the water you can

1 teaspoon whole fennel seed, lightly crushed

1 teaspoon Italian seasoning

2 teaspoons dried parsley flakes

1 teaspoon ground black pepper

1 teaspoon salt

1/2 teaspoon dried basil

1/2 teaspoon dried thyme leaf

1 egg

5 cups Marinara sauce, homemade (recipe page 158) or store bought

9 ounces lasagna noodles (about 7 or 8), uncooked*

1-1/2 pounds Italian sausage, hot or mild, removed from casings, cooked and drained

1/2 pound grated mozzarella

1/2 cup grated Parmesan

HELPFUL HINT: I know Jim thought I was crazy the first time he saw me make this with uncooked noodles, but the lasagna noodles will cook inside the dish. If you want to precook them, you may but it's not necessary.

1. Preheat oven to 350 degrees F.

2. Combine the ricotta, Parmesan, spinach, spices and egg in a mixing bowl and mix well.

3. Spread 1 cup of marinara sauce in the bottom of a 13x9-inch deep walled baking dish. Add a layer of lasagna noodles, about half of them, uncooked, on top of the sauce. Add 2 more cups of marinara over the raw noodles. Divide the ricotta cheese mixture in half and crumble one half of the mixture over the marinara. Top the cheese mixture with half of the cooked sausage. Top the sausage with 1/2 cup of Parmesan cheese.

4. Repeat layers beginning with a layer of uncooked noodles, 2 cups marinara, the other half of ricotta cheese mixture, the rest of the Italian sausage, 1/2 cup Parmesan.
    continued on page 116...

HELPFUL HINT: Precook noodles if using store bought sauce.

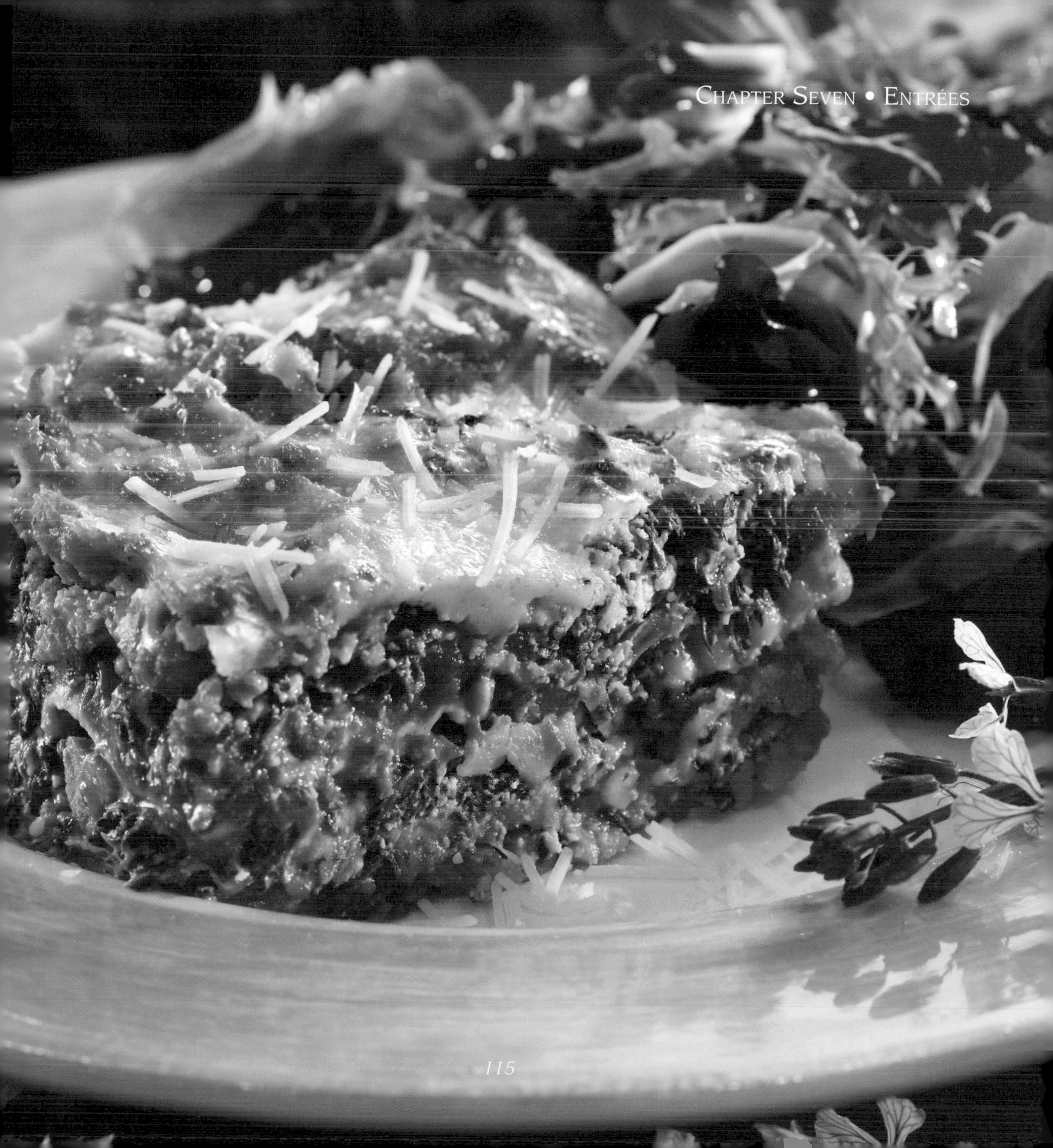

Italian Sausage Lasagna

...continued from page 114

5. Top with grated mozzarella cheese. Cover with aluminum foil, wrap tightly. Bake covered at 350 degrees F for 90 minutes. Allow lasagna to stand for 10 minutes before slicing.
   Serves 12

Variations:

FOR VEGGIE LASAGNA:
Substitute 2 pounds sautéed sliced zucchini for the Italian sausage.

FOR MEDITERRANEAN LASAGNA:
Replace the Italian sausage with the ingredients at left and add 8 ounces of feta cheese to the mozzarella

1. Melt butter in a skillet.

2. Add remaining ingredients and cook together until soft, about 8 minutes.

MEDITERRANEAN LASAGNA
4 tablespoons butter

4 leeks, washed, sliced

10 cloves garlic, peeled, chopped

1-1/2 pounds mushrooms, sliced

1/2 cup sun-dried tomatoes, chopped

1/2 cup roasted red peppers, chopped

1 cup sliced Kalamata olives

2, 6-ounce jars marinated artichoke hearts, chopped

1 tablespoon all-purpose seasoning such as Cahoots House Rub

Grilled Chicken with Mediterranean Relish

This is a simple preparation with beautiful and delicious results, and is great for either a casual backyard barbeque or a special occasion luncheon.

FOR THE CHICKEN:

1/2 cup olive oil

1/2 cup garlic, chopped

2 tablespoons seasoned rice wine vinegar

2 tablespoons fresh lime juice

2 teaspoons salt

8, 7-ounce chicken breasts, boneless, skin on

1. Combine the olive oil, garlic, seasoned rice wine vinegar, lime juice and salt in a medium stainless steel bowl. Add chicken breast and coat well. Marinate for 1-1/2 hours.

2. Prepare a charcoal or gas grill. Grill chicken over a medium-high heat about 10-12 minutes, turning twice until the chicken is marked well with char marks and done (160 degrees F. internal temperature).

3. Place chicken on a serving platter and spoon the relish down the center of the chicken breasts and serve.
   Serves 8

FOR THE MEDITERRANEAN RELISH:

1 red and 1 yellow bell pepper, roasted and peeled

1/2 cup sliced black olives

2 cloves garlic, minced

1 tablespoon white balsamic vinegar

2 teaspoons crushed red peppers

1/2 cup fresh parsley, chopped

1 tablespoon honey

1/3 cup olive oil

salt and pepper

1. Mix all the ingredients together in a medium bowl.

ADVANCE PREPARATION:
The Mediterranean relish can be made up to 2 days ahead and refrigerated.

WINE SUGGESTION:
Chardonnay, Roussanne or Syrah

Soy & Ginger Marinated Pork Tenderloin with Mango Avocado Salsa

This is yet another hit from our barbeque menu and is a fresh addition to summer gatherings. It goes great with our Coconut Ginger Rice (page 86).

2 tablespoons honey

2 tablespoons Dijon mustard

2 tablespoons toasted sesame oil

2 tablespoons seasoned rice vinegar

2 tablespoons fresh ginger, chopped

1 tablespoon soy sauce

1 tablespoon fresh garlic, chopped

2 pork tenderloins

1. Combine all ingredients except the pork in a stainless steel or glass bowl (or large recloseable plastic bag).

2. Add pork tenderloins to the marinade and coat well. Cover and refrigerate. Marinate at least 6 hours or overnight.

3. Prepare a charcoal or gas fire. Grill the tenderloin over medium-high heat until the internal temperature is 155 degrees F, about 20 minutes. Remove from grill and let rest for 10 minutes. The center should be slightly pink. Serve with Mango Avocado Salsa.
Serves 8-10

FOR THE MANGO AVOCADO SALSA:

1 pound mango, fresh or frozen, coarsely chopped

1 avocado, diced

1 red bell pepper, diced

1/4 cup cilantro, chopped

2 green onions

3 tablespoons orange juice

3 tablespoons lime juice

1 tablespoon brown sugar

1 teaspoon ground ginger

1. Mix all ingredients together.

WINE SUGGESTION:
Pinot Blanc, Viognier, dry Riesling or dry Gewurztraminer

Citrus & Chardonnay Marinated Grilled Turkey Breast

This recipe is always a winner at our barbeque events. It's out of the ordinary, but very easy to do and leftovers – if you have any – make great sandwiches. We always use Chardonnay for the marinade, but you could use any white varietal.

6-8 pound boneless turkey breast

1 cup orange juice

1 cup lime juice

1 cup lemon juice

1 cup chardonnay

1 cup olive oil

1/2 cup granulated garlic

1/4 cup Cahoots House Rub or other all purpose seasoning

1. Rinse turkey breast under cold water and place in a large stainless steel bowl. Mix together the remaining ingredients, and pour over the turkey breast. Marinate for 4-6 hours, but do not over marinate since the citrus juices will start to "cook" the meat.

2. Prepare charcoal or gas grill. Over medium-high heat, cook turkey breast, turning as needed, until internal temperature reaches 160 degrees F., about 45 minutes. Take your time so you don't char the meat.

3. Let rest for about 10 minutes. Slice and serve with salsa or Cahoots Chipotle sauce.
   Serves 8-10

WINE SUGGESTION: Chardonnay or Roussanne

Roast Chicken with Garlic Herb Butter & Vegetables

There is nothing like the classic roasted chicken, especially when accompanied with aromatic herbs and great vegetables for a satisfying crowd-pleasing meal. Leftovers are always a win-win too!

1/4 pound unsalted butter (1 stick), softened

1/3 cup chopped fresh herbs, any combination of parsley, rosemary, thyme, chives, or oregano.

10 cloves garlic, minced

1/4 cup Dijon mustard

1 teaspoon salt

1 teaspoon black pepper

1, 5-6 pound roasting chicken

1 pound baby carrots

1 pound cippollini onions, trimmed and peeled

1 pound baby potatoes, or larger ones cut in 1/2

1. Preheat oven to 400 degrees F.

2. Combine the butter, chopped herbs, garlic, Dijon, salt and pepper.

3. Slide your fingers between the chicken breast meat and the skin, loosening the skin. Spread half the butter mixture under the skin onto the breast meat.

4. Melt the remaining herb butter, reserving about 2 tablespoons to brush over the top of the chicken, and add the vegetables. Toss until well coated.

5. Place the chicken in a large roasting pan. Arrange the vegetables around the chicken. Brush with remaining 2 tablespoons of herb butter. Sprinkle with salt and pepper. Roast chicken at 400 degrees F. for about 2 hours until golden brown and a thermometer inserted into the thickest part of the thigh reaches 180 degrees F. Transfer the chicken and vegetables to serving platter.

Serves 6

HELPFUL HINT: Boiler Onions can be substituted for the cippollini onions.

WINE SUGGESTION:
Chardonnay or Pinot Noir

Enchiladas

The secret to these enchiladas is the sauce. You can use shredded chicken, shredded beef, roasted vegetables or just cheese. We can't tell you how many people purchase pans of our enchiladas and pass them off as their own. Hey why not? We'll never tell! You'll also have enough sauce left over to freeze for another batch.

1/4 cup corn or vegetable oil

10 corn tortillas

1 recipe enchilada sauce, (recipe page 159)

3/4 pound (about 3 cups) cooked shredded chicken, beef or roasted chopped vegetables for filling

3 bunches green onions, washed, sliced and divided

1 pound shredded jack/ cheddar cheese blend (or 1/2 pound of each)

sour cream and salsa as desired for garnish

BEVERAGE SUGGESTION:
Ice cold beer, Zinfandel or Tempranillo

1. Preheat oven to 350 degrees F. Spray a 13x9x2-inch baking dish with non-stick spray.

2. In a medium sauté pan, heat corn oil over medium-high heat. When the oil is hot, sauté corn tortillas quickly, about 10 seconds per side to soften. Drain on paper towels.

3. Mix 1 cup of enchilada sauce with the shredded meat or vegetables.

4. Spoon a 1/2 cup of enchilada sauce onto a large rimmed plate. Add a sautéed tortilla to the sauce. Turn to coat.

5. Place about 1/3 cup of filling on the coated tortilla. Sprinkle with about 1 tablespoon of chopped green onion. Then top with about 2 tablespoons shredded cheese. Roll up and place seam side down in baking dish. Repeat until all 8 tortillas are filled. You should have 2 rows of 4 enchiladas, side-by-side on the long horizontal side of the dish.

6. Top the enchiladas with about 1 cup additional enchilada sauce. Top with 1 cup additional cheese and remaining chopped green onions.

7. Bake, covered, at 350 degrees F. for about 35-45 minutes. Serve with sour cream and salsa.
Serves 6-8

Mediterranean Turkey Meatloaf with Cabernet Ketchup

This is great on its own as an entrée but we like it best re-warmed in a sandwich on sourdough bread with crisp lettuce and lots of mayonnaise. This is also known as a "Franwich," named after Lisa's mother Fran.

4 tablespoons butter

4 cloves garlic, minced

1 yellow onion, diced

1 leek, sliced and washed

1 stalk celery, chopped

1 carrot, chopped

2 teaspoons salt

1/2 teaspoon black pepper

2 tablespoons dried parsley

1/2 teaspoon dried thyme leaves

1/2 teaspoon dried oregano

1 teaspoon Italian seasoning

1 tablespoon Worcestershire sauce

1/4 cup sun-dried tomatoes in oil, drained and chopped

1 roasted red bell pepper, peeled and chopped

2 eggs

1 cup fresh bread crumbs

1/3 cup pine nuts, lightly toasted

2 pounds ground turkey

1/2 cup ketchup

1/2 cup Cabernet

1. Preheat oven to 350 degrees F (325 convection). Spray or lightly butter 9x9-inch square baking dish.

2. Melt butter in a sauté pan over medium-high heat. Add garlic, onion and leek. Cook until soft, about 5 minutes. Add celery and carrot and continue cooking for another 4-5 minutes.

3. Transfer vegetable mixture to a large mixing bowl, and add the herbs and spices, Worcestershire sauce, sun-dried tomatoes, roasted red bell pepper, eggs, bread crumbs, pine nuts and ground turkey. Mix well.

4. Spoon meatloaf mixture into baking dish.

5. Mix together the ketchup and red wine in a small bowl. Pour over the top of the meatloaf.

6. Bake at 350 degrees F. for 45-50 minutes.
   Serves 6 to 8 with leftovers for sandwiches

Herb Pesto Crusted Rack of Lamb

This recipe is excellent as an entrée but is also great as an appetizer. We usually serve "Frenched" lamb racks, meaning that the butcher (or one of us!) has cut away all the meat and fat from between the rib bones. It leaves a rich eye of meat and makes for an elegant presentation

FOR THE HERB PESTO:

1 cup onion, chopped

1/4 cup Dijon mustard

1 cup fresh parsley, minced

1 cup fresh basil

2 tablespoons fresh chives

2 tablespoons fresh oregano

2 tablespoons fresh mint

2 tablespoons fresh rosemary, minced

6 cloves garlic, minced

1 lemon, zested, juiced

1/2 cup olive oil

1 teaspoon salt

1 teaspoon pepper

FOR THE LAMB:

4 lamb racks, frenched

salt and pepper

1/4 cup olive oil

1. Mix all pesto ingredients in a food processor or blender and blend until smooth. Set aside.

2. Preheat oven to 450 degrees F.

3. Heat 1/4 cup olive oil in a large sauté pan over medium high heat.

4. Salt and pepper the lamb racks. Working in batches, add the racks to the hot oil. Sear the lamb racks for about 3 minutes a side. Remove from pan and set aside.

5. Once all the racks are seared, cover each rack with about 3/4 cup of the herb pesto and set in a baking pan.

6. Bake at 450 degrees F. for about 10-12 minutes or until the internal temperature reaches 130 degrees F.

7. Let lamb rest for a few minutes, then slice into individual chops and serve.
   Serves 6, or 12-14 as an appetizer

WINE SUGGESTION:
Syrah or Pinot Noir

Salmon Crusted with Cashew, Fennel & Basil

We try and buy wild or line-caught salmon whenever possible. The wild salmon season typically runs from May through September. You can often tell the difference from wild salmon and farm-raised by looking at it; unless it's been altered with food coloring, farm-raised salmon is usually lighter pink color with obvious white stripes that are actually fat marbling, running through the flesh where as wild salmon is usually very deep pink without the white stripes. Most reputable fish markets and grocery stores will label their salmon.

6, 5- or 6-ounce individual portions of salmon (approx. 1-inch thick), skin off and pin bones removed*

2 teaspoons Cahoots House Rub or other all purpose seasoning or salt and pepper

2 cups cashews, roasted and salted

1 ounce fresh basil leaves

1 tablespoon fennel seed, crushed or chopped in a spice grinder

1. Preheat oven to 400 degrees F. Spray a rimmed baking sheet with non-stick spray.

2. Place salmon filet or individual portions on the prepared baking sheet. Season the fish with the rub or other seasonings.

3. In the work bowl of a food processor fitted with a steel blade add the cashews, basil and fennel seeds. Pulse the processor until the mixture is combined into a coarse mixture.

4. Spread the cashew mixture onto the fish, firmly patting it in place.

5. Bake at 400 degrees F for 14-16 minutes.
   Serves 6

*This recipe also works well with a whole 2-pound salmon filet, baked for about 30-35 minutes.

WINE SUGGESTION:
Pinot Noir or a light red Rhône blend

Cioppino

This is a wonderful meal for a cool night (preferably at the coast), with a crisp green salad and lots and lots of garlic bread.

1/2 cup olive oil

8 cloves garlic, chopped

2 yellow onions, chopped

6 stalks celery, chopped, about 3 cups

1 carrot, diced

3 bell peppers, chopped, preferably 1 green, 1 yellow, 1 red

3 cups clam juice

4, 28-ounce cans whole peeled tomatoes

2, 28-ounce cans tomato sauce

1-1/2 cups dry red wine

2 tablespoons Italian seasoning

1/2 cup fresh parsley, chopped

1 tablespoon salt

1/2 tablespoon black pepper

2 bay leaves

1 tablespoon crushed red pepper

3 dashes of hot sauce

36 little neck clams, about 3 pounds, washed

2 pounds large shrimp, shelled, deveined

2 pounds firm white fish, such as cod, cut into 1-inch pieces

2 pounds sea scallops

1 pound crab legs, Dungeness or snow crab

1. Heat olive oil over medium heat in a 10-quart stock pot. Add garlic and onions and cook until soft, about 5 minutes. Add the celery, carrot, and bell peppers and cook for a few minutes more.

2. Add clam juice, tomatoes, tomato sauce, red wine, Italian seasoning, parsley, salt, pepper, bay leaves, red pepper and hot sauce. Let simmer, covered for about 1 hour.

3. When you are ready to serve, bring Cioppino sauce up to a low boil. Add the clams. Let cook for about 5 minutes or until the clams start to open. Add the shrimp, fish, scallops and crab legs. Turn the heat down to low and simmer until heated through, about 4 minutes. Ladle into big soup bowls and serve with lots of garlic bread.
Serves 14-16

WINE SUGGESTION:
Pinot Noir, Zinfandel or
Sangiovese

Halibut with Citrus Butter & Macadamia Nuts

If you ask us, this is how halibut should be served – great citrus flavors, rich crunchy nuts, and the flavors allow the fish to shine through. So decadent!

1/2 cup unsalted butter, softened

zest of 1 orange plus the juice of half of an orange

zest of 2 lemons plus the juice of one lemon

zest of 2 limes plus the juice of 1 lime

1/2 teaspoon salt

1/4 teaspoon chili powder

8, 5- or 6-ounce halibut filets (approx. 1-inch thick)

2 cups raw macadamia nuts, coarsely chopped

1. Preheat oven to 400 degrees F.

2. Cream together butter, citrus zests, salt and chili powder in a small bowl. It will take a little time, but the juices will combine with the butter.

3. Season halibut filets with Cahoots House Rub or salt and pepper. Spread about 2 tablespoons of the citrus butter onto each filet and place them on a baking sheet. Sprinkle with chopped nuts.

4. Bake at 400 degrees for about 14-16 minutes. After 14-16 minutes the nuts should be lightly toasted and the fish should be soft to the touch when done. Be careful not to overcook this delicate fish.
Serves 8

Wine suggestion:
Big buttery Chardonnay,
Pinot Blanc or Viognier

Bacon-Wrapped Beef Tenderloin with Gorgonzola Mushroom Sauce

You can't go wrong with this one – what's not to like? We also used a similar sauce on our Cahoots Club Cobb sandwich in the café. It was the "bomb."

FOR THE GORGONZOLA MUSHROOM SAUCE:
4 tablespoons unsalted butter

1-1/2 cups green onions, chopped

1/2 pound mushrooms, sliced

2 cups Gorgonzola cheese, crumbled

FOR THE BEEF:
8, 5-ounce center-cut beef tenderloins

8 slices good quality bacon

Cahoots House Rub or other favorite seasoning

1. Melt butter over medium heat in small sauté pan.

2. Add onion and mushrooms and sauté until soft and tender, about 3 minutes. Add cheese and stir until melted.

3. Prepare a gas or charcoal fire or grill pan.

4. Wrap a piece of bacon around each filet and secure with a toothpick. Season each filet with Cahoots House Rub or other favorite seasoning.

5. Grill filets over medium-high heat, turning twice, until done, approximately 15 minutes, or until the internal temperature is 140 degrees F. for medium rare. Allow meat to rest 10 minutes. Remove picks before serving.

6. Serve with Gorgonzola Mushroom sauce.
   Serves 8

CHAPTER SEVEN • ENTRÉES

WINE SUGGESTION:
Petite Sirah,
Cabernet Sauvignon or
Meritage

131

CHAPTER EIGHT

Desserts

Carrot Cake

We have made so many variations of carrot cake over the years – including jalapeño carrot cake with margarita cream cheese frosting! – but this recipe has been the simplest and most popular over the years.

2 cups all purpose flour

2 teaspoons baking soda

1-1/2 teaspoons salt

1-1/2 tablespoons cinnamon

2 cups sugar

6 eggs

1 cup corn oil

1 pound carrots, peeled and grated

1. Preheat oven to 325 degrees F (300 convection). Prepare 3 9-inch cake pans with non stick spray or butter and lightly flour them.

2. Sift together flour, baking soda, salt and cinnamon. Stir in sugar and set aside.

3. In a mixing bowl, beat the eggs until frothy. Slowly add the oil and continue mixing until incorporated. Slowly add flour mixture and mix until smooth, then add the grated carrots and mix until blended.

4. Divide the batter evenly between the 3 prepared cake pans. Bake for 35 minutes or until the cake springs back when lightly touched. Cool cakes.

5. When cakes are cool enough to handle remove from pans and frost.

FOR THE CREAM CHEESE FROSTING:

1 pound cream cheese, softened

1 stick unsalted butter (1/4 pound) softened

3 cups powdered sugar, sifted

2 teaspoons vanilla extract

1/2 cup walnuts, toasted and chopped

Cream Cheese Frosting

1. Beat together cream cheese and butter in a mixing bowl.

2. Add powdered sugar and vanilla. Mix until blended.

3. Frost one layer of cake, sprinkle with 2 tablespoons of chopped nuts. Repeat with the next two layers then frost sides. Sprinkle with remaining walnuts.
Serves 10 to 12

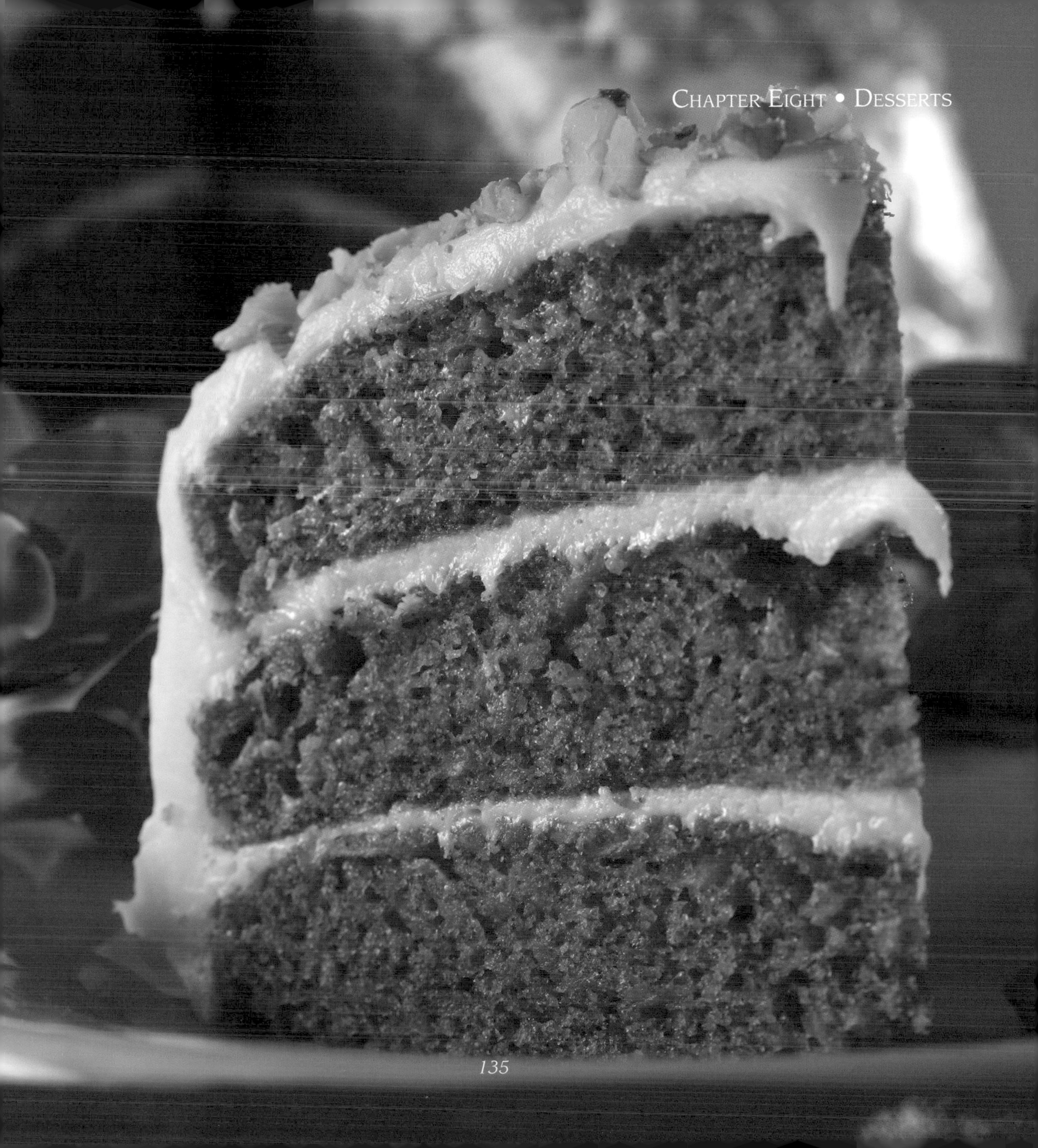

Streusel Apple Pie

With so many layers of flavors, this pie exceeds your expectations for regular apple pie. Every summer I anxiously await the Granny Smith apples ripening in the orchard while visions of this pie dance in my head.

FOR THE CRUST:

1-1/2 cups all purpose flour

3 tablespoons sugar

1 teaspoon cinnamon

1/2 teaspoon salt

1/2 cup unsalted butter, very cold or partially frozen

1/3 cup cold water

FOR THE FILLING:

8 Granny Smith apples, peeled, cored and sliced

1-1/2 cups sour cream

1 cup sugar

1/3 cup flour

1 egg, beaten

2 teaspoons vanilla

1/2 teaspoon salt

1. Preheat oven to 400 degrees F.

2. Add flour, sugar, cinnamon and salt to the bowl of a food processor fitted with the steel blade. Pulse a few times to mix. Cut butter into 10-12 uniform sized pieces and add to the food processor.

3. Pulse the mixture to cut the butter and flour mixture until it resembles a coarse crumbs. With the motor continuously running, add the water and blend until the dough comes off the sides of the bowl and forms a ball.

4. Remove the dough from the processor and shape into a ball, flatten slightly and let it rest for about 10 minutes before rolling.

5. Roll out dough on a floured surface and line a 10-inch deep dish pie pan with the pastry.

6. Combine all filling ingredients in a bowl.

7. Spoon filling into the pie crust and bake for 10 minutes. Reduce heat to 350 and bake for an additional 40 minutes. While the pie is baking make the streusel topping (page 137).

8. After the 40 minutes is up, remove pie from the oven and sprinkle with the streusel topping. Return to the oven and bake for an additional 15 minutes. Let rest for about 15 minutes and serve.

Serves 8-10

FOR THE STREUSEL TOPPING:

1 cup walnuts

1/2 cup flour

1/3 cup brown sugar

1 tablespoon cinnamon

pinch of salt

1/2 cup unsalted butter, very cold or partially frozen, cut into 10-12 uniform pieces.

1. Add all the streusel topping ingredients to a food processor fitted with the steel blade and pulse the machine until the mixture is coarse and crumbly.

Wild Berry Blondies

Do blondes really have more fun? We took the chocolate out of the brownie and you can't argue wth the result. This amazing bar cookie is addicting.

2 cups all purpose flour

1 teaspoon baking powder

1/4 teaspoon baking soda

1 teaspoon salt

1/2 cup (1 stick) unsalted butter, softened

2 cups brown sugar

2 eggs

2 teaspoons vanilla extract

1 cup almonds, coarsely chopped

1-1/2 pints mixed fresh berries: blueberries, raspberries and blackberries

1. Preheat oven to 325 degrees F (300 convection). Butter a 13x9x2-inch baking dish and lightly dust it with flour.

2. Sift together the 2 cups flour, baking powder, baking soda and salt in a mixing bowl.

3. In a separate bowl, beat the butter and brown sugar until fluffy. Beat in eggs one at a time. Add vanilla and blend. Add flour mixture and beat until blended. Stir in almonds.

4. Spoon batter into prepared pan and spread out evenly. Top with mixed berries.

5. Bake for about 50-60 minutes until golden and tooth pick inserted into the center comes out clean.
Makes 12 (3-inch x 3-inch) or 24 (2-inch x 2-inch) squares

Chocolate Raspberry Croissant Bread Pudding

For our winemaker dinners, we are constantly working on chocolate desserts that pair well with wine. This one was a big hit at Opolo Vineyards' Wine Festival dinner paired with their Mountain Zinfandel.

2 tablespoons unsalted butter, melted

3-1/2 cups half & half

2 tablespoons Grand Marnier®

1-1/2 cups dark chocolate, chopped

1/3 cup brown sugar, packed

1 tablespoon cocoa powder

7 eggs

2 teaspoons vanilla extract
pinch of salt

10 large croissants, day old, cut into 1-inch cubes

3 cups dark chocolate, chopped

1 pint fresh raspberries, plus extra for garnish

whipped cream for garnish

1. Preheat oven to 350 degrees F (325 convection). Brush a 13 x 9 x 2 inch baking dish with the 2 tablespoons of melted butter.

2. Warm the half & half and Grand Marnier® in a medium saucepan until it begins to simmer. Stir in chopped chocolate. Remove from heat and let sit for 1 minute. Whisk in brown sugar and cocoa powder and mix well. Set aside to cool for about 15 minutes.

3. In a separate bowl, whip the eggs, vanilla and salt. Gradually whisk in the chocolate mixture.

4. Spread half of the croissant cubes over the bottom of the prepared pan. Sprinkle 2 cups of the chopped chocolate over the croissants. Top the chocolate with the remaining half of croissant cubes and remaining chopped chocolate.

5. Pour chocolate egg mixture over croissant cubes and chocolate. Top with fresh raspberries. Bake for 20 minutes.

6. Serve with a lightly sweetened whipped cream and additional fresh raspberries.
Serves 12 -14

WINE SUGGESTION:
Fruity Zinfandel, late harvest Zinfandel or a Kir Royal made with Chambord® or another raspberry-flavored liqueur.

Cold Lemon Soufflé

This is a refreshing and unique dessert. Since it's light and airy, it's nice to serve after a heavy meal. We like to ream out lemon halves, trim a thin slice off the bottom and fill them with the soufflé as individual treats.

5 eggs, separated*

1-1/2 cups sugar

2 tablespoons unflavored gelatin

3 lemons, zested (grated rinds) and juiced, plus 1/2 cup lemon juice

1-1/2 cups heavy cream

*This recipe does have raw egg in it, so be sure to keep it well chilled.

1. Butter and lightly sugar a 6-cup soufflé dish.

2. Beat together the egg yolks and sugar until they are a pale yellow color.

3. In a small sauce pan, add the gelatin to the lemon juice and zest and let sit 5 minutes. Heat mixture over medium heat until the gelatin is completely dissolved. Remove from heat and cool 1-2 minutes. Stir into the egg yolk mixture.

4. Beat heavy cream until it forms soft peaks. Fold into the lemon-yolk mixture.

5. Beat egg whites until stiff. Fold into lemon-yolk-cream mixture. Pour into the prepared soufflé dish and chill for at least 2 hours or overnight.
   Serves 6-8

NOTE: Raw egg preparations are generally considered safe for healthy adults, when handled with care. See page 171 for safe egg handling practices.

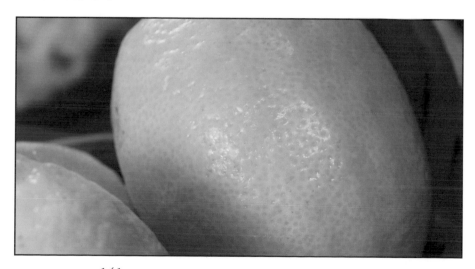

Lemon Squares

This is a classic dessert that never seems to go out of style. You can also alter the flavor a bit by using Key Lime juice instead of lemon.

FOR THE CRUST:
2-1/4 cups all purpose flour

1/2 cup powdered sugar

1 cup unsalted butter, very cold or partially frozen, cut into uniform pieces

FOR THE FILLING:
7 eggs

3 tablespoons all purpose flour

1 teaspoon baking powder

1/2 cup lemon juice

2-3/4 cups sugar

powdered sugar for decoration

1. Preheat oven to 325 degrees F (300 convection).

2. Add flour and powdered sugar to the work bowl of a food processor fitted with the steel blade. Pulse a few times to mix. Add butter pieces and mix until crumbly.

3. Press the flour mixture into the bottom of a 13x9x2-inch baking dish. Bake at 350 degrees F for 15 minutes.

4. Combine eggs, flour, baking powder, lemon juice and sugar, and mix well.

5. Pour the lemon mixture over the prepared crust. Bake at 350 degrees F for 30 minutes or until golden brown.

6. Cool completely before cutting. Dust with powdered sugar. **Makes 12 (3-inch x 3-inch) squares or 24 (2-inch x 2-inch) squares**

Chocolate Decadence

If you love chocolate this should be right up your alley! It's not really a cake, or mousse or flourless chocolate cake, but it is decadent. I like to use bittersweet chocolate, but feel free to use your favorite chocolate.

FOR THE CAKE:

1 pound good quality dark chocolate, chopped

6 ounces unsalted butter

1/4 cup flour

1 teaspoon vanilla extract

5 eggs

1/2 cup sugar

FOR THE GANACHE FROSTING:

1-1/2 cups good quality dark chocolate, chopped

1/2 cup heavy cream

1 egg yolk

1/2 teaspoon vanilla

NOTE: "Ganache" is a French term referring to a smooth mixture of chopped chocolate and heavy cream.

1. Preheat the oven to 325 degrees F (300 convection).

2. Melt chocolate and butter together in a double boiler until smooth. Stir in flour and vanilla. Set aside.

3. Beat together the eggs and sugar with an electric mixer until pale yellow and thick. Fold a small amount of the egg mixture into the chocolate mixture, then gently fold the chocolate mixture into the egg mixture. Pour batter into a 9-inch spring-form pan.

4. Bake at 350 degrees F for 45 minutes. Remove from the oven and allow the cake to cool.

5. While the cake is baking, prepare the ganache. Heat the cream over medium heat in a small sauce pan until it just begins to simmer.

6. Add chocolate. Remove from the heat and stir until the chocolate is melted. Add the egg yolk and vanilla until blended.

7. Remove the springform pan by carefully sliding a knife around the outside edge between the side of the pan and the cake and release the buckle. Pour the ganache frosting over the top, letting it drip over the sides.
Serves 10-12

Wine suggestion:
Late harvest Zinfandel, late
harvest Barbera or port

Chocolate Peanut Butterfinger® Cheesecake

I have lost count on how many different cheesecake combinations we have come up with over the years but this one combines the always popular peanut butter and chocolate and one of my favorites – Butterfinger® bars.

FOR THE CRUST:
1-1/2 cups chocolate graham cracker crumbs

1 tablespoon sugar

4 tablespoons butter, melted

2 full-size Butterfinger® bars, broken into pieces

FOR THE FILLING:
1-1/2 pounds cream cheese, softened

1 cup sugar

3 eggs

12 ounces semi sweet chocolate, melted

1 teaspoon vanilla extract

2 tablespoons cocoa powder

1/2 cup sour cream

1 cup chunky peanut butter

FOR THE GARNISH:
1 full-size Butterfinger® bar, broken into pieces

whipped cream

1. Combine the chocolate graham cracker crumbs, sugar and melted butter and press into the bottom of a 9-inch springform pan. Top the crust with two of the broken Butterfinger® bars.

2. Preheat oven to 350 degrees F.

3. Combine the cream cheese and sugar and mix in a mixing bowl or food processor.

4. Add the eggs and to the cream cheese and sugar mixture, blend until combined, scraping down the sides of the mixing bowl or food processor until smooth. Add melted chocolate, vanilla, cocoa powder and sour cream. Blend until smooth. Add peanut butter and blend until combined; be careful not to over mix.

5. Pour filling into prepared crust. Bake at 350 degrees F in the middle of the oven for 50 minutes or until just set. Turn off the oven and prop the oven door open to allow the cheesecake to cool slowly, about 15 minutes. Remove the cheesecake from the oven and chill for several hours or overnight. Remove the springform pan by carefully sliding a knife around the outside edge between the side of the pan and the cake and release the buckle.

6. Decorate with broken Butterfinger® bar and whipped cream.
Serves 14-16

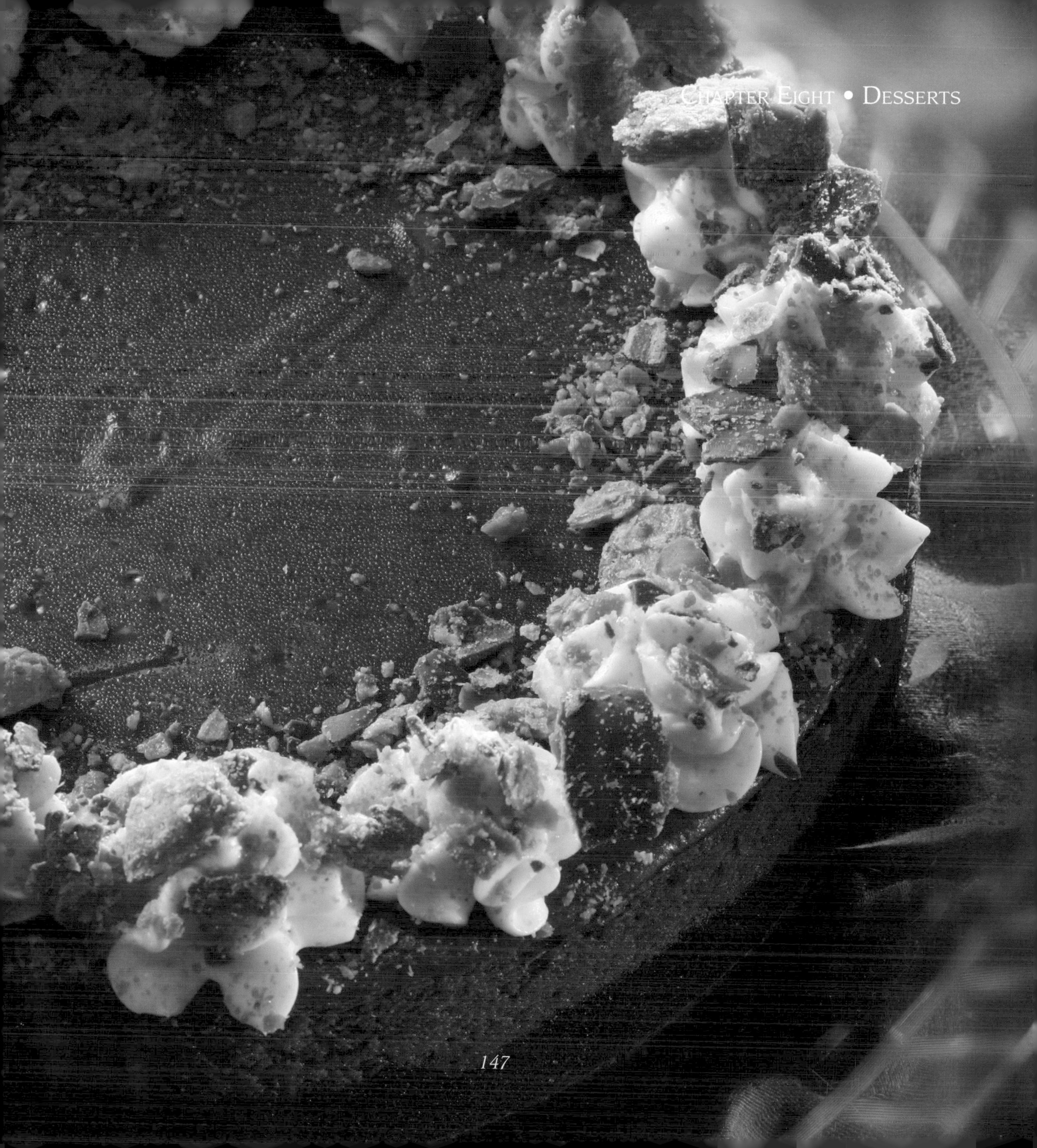

Lemon Parfait with Blueberries & Grand Marnier® Whipped Cream

This is as delicious as it is beautiful. Feel free to substitute different berries or mixed berries into the recipe.

Lemon Curd (recipe follows)

Grand Marnier® Whipped Cream (recipe follows)

2 pints fresh blueberries

FOR THE LEMON CURD:
4 eggs & 8 egg yolks

1-1/2 cup sugar

1 cup lemon juice

zest from 4 lemons

1 cup unsalted butter cut into about 8-10 pieces

FOR THE GRAND MARNIER® WHIPPED CREAM:
2 cups heavy cream

1/4 cup powdered sugar

2 Tablespoons Grand Marnier® or other orange flavored liqueur

1. Combine eggs and egg yolks in a medium sauce pan. Add sugar, lemon juice and lemon zest. Cook over medium-low heat, stirring constantly until the mixture thickens and coats the back of a spoon, about 10 minutes.

2. Remove from heat and add the butter pieces a few at a time, stirring to incorporate into a smooth mixture.

3. Place lemon curd mixture in a bowl. Cover and chill for about an hour.

4. Combine all three Grand Marnier® Whipped Cream ingredients in a mixing bowl and whip until soft peaks form.

5. To assemble, start with 4-6 parfait glasses. Spoon about 1/4 cup whipped cream into the bottom of each glass. Top whipped cream with 2 tablespoons of blueberries. Top the blueberries with 1/3 cup of lemon curd.

6. Repeat layers 3 times finishing with whipped cream and blueberries.
Serves 4-6 depending on the size of parfait glasses

Tiramisu Cheesecake

"Tiramisu" translates to "carry me up" or "pick me up." It is traditionally made with lady fingers or sponge cake that have been soaked in a coffee and Marsala mixture then layered with Mascarpone cheese, whipped cream and chopped chocolate. I came up with this variation for two reasons: it's a simple assembly and it holds better than traditional Tiramisu. I also use Kahlua in place of Marsala.

FOR THE CRUST:

1-1/2 cups chocolate cookie crumbs

1 tablespoon sugar

4 tablespoons butter, melted

FOR THE FILLING:

1-1/2 pound cream cheese, softened

1 cup sugar

3 eggs plus 1 egg yolk

1 teaspoon vanilla

1-1/2 cups mascarpone, softened

1-1/2 cups Kahlua®

1-1/2 cups brewed espresso coffee, cooled

30 ladyfingers

2 cups semi-sweet chocolate, chopped

1/4 cup cocoa powder

whipped cream and fresh berries for garnish

1. Combine all the ingredients in a small bowl, and press the mixture into the bottom of a 9-inch springform pan.

1. Preheat oven to 350 degrees F.

3. Combine the cream cheese and sugar and mix in a mixing bowl or food processor. Add eggs and egg yolk and blend until combined, scraping down the sides of the mixing bowl or food processor until smooth. Add vanilla and mascarpone and blend until smooth; be careful not to over mix. Set aside.

4. Mix the Kahlua® and coffee together. Dip the ladyfingers into the coffee mixture and lay them on top of the cookie crust in the springform pan, in a single layer.

5. Top the ladyfingers with 1 cup of chopped chocolate.

6. Pour half of the cheesecake batter over the chopped chocolate.

7. Repeat the layers again with the ladyfingers, chopped chocolate and the rest of the batter. Bake in the middle of the oven at 350 degrees F for 30 minutes or until just set. Turn off the oven and prop the oven door open to allow the cheesecake to cool slowly to avoid surface cracks, about 15 minutes.

8. Remove the cheesecake from the oven and chill for at least 6 hours or overnight. Remove the springform pan by carefully sliding a knife around the outside edge between the side of the pan and the cake and release the buckle. Dust the cheesecake with sifted cocoa powder, serve with whipped cream and fresh berries.
Serves 14-16

HELPFUL HINT: Slightly warming the bottom of the springform over a gas flame will help the cheesecake to slide off the pan onto a cake board or serving dish.

When pairing wine with dessert you want to be sure that the dessert is not sweeter than the wine. I will often use less sugar in a dessert to help match it with a specific wine.

ADVANCE PREPARATION: can be made a day ahead.

WINE SUGGESTION: Late harvest Zinfandel, Port or Vin Santo

CHAPTER NINE

Basics

Pâte Brisée
(Pastry Crust)

There are variables to making pastry dough: humidity, altitude, and room temperature. If your dough is too soft, you can roll it out using extra flour. I use frozen butter to offset the heat that is generated by the blade of the food processor.

1-1/2 cups all purpose flour

1/2 teaspoon salt

1 teaspoon sugar

1 stick, 4 ounces, unsalted butter cut into 1/2-inch cubes and frozen

1/3 cup very cold water

1. Add flour, salt and sugar to a food processor fitted with the steel blade. Pulse a couple of times to mix.

2. Add the frozen butter. Turn on processor and pulse, allowing it to cut the butter and flour together (about 30 seconds) until the mixture resembles coarse meal.

3. With the machine running, add cold water until the dough comes together and forms a ball.

Pesto

Basil pesto is the classic version, but with so many cultural influences especially here in California, pesto can take on many more flavors.

Basil Pesto

2 cups fresh basil leaves, packed

4 cloves garlic, chopped

1/3 cup pine nuts

1 cup Parmesan cheese, grated

1/2 cup olive oil

salt and pepper to taste

1. Add basil, garlic, pine nuts, and Parmesan cheese to a blender or food processor.

2. With the motor running, add the olive oil in a steady stream until blended.

3. Add salt and pepper to taste.

Cilantro Pesto

3 cloves garlic, chopped

3 cups fresh cilantro leaves, loosely packed

1/4 cup pine nuts

1/2 teaspoon each salt and pepper or to taste

1/4 cup mild olive oil

1. Add the garlic, cilantro, pine nuts, salt and pepper to a blender or food processor.

2. With the motor running add the olive oil in a steady stream until blended.

3. Add salt and pepper to taste.

Sun-dried Tomato Pesto

1 cup sun-dried tomatoes in oil, drained, roughly chopped

1/2 cup fresh basil, packed

1/2 cup Parmesan cheese, grated

1/4 cup pine nuts

3 cloves garlic, peeled, chopped

1/2-3/4 cup extra virgin olive oil

salt and pepper to taste

1. Add tomatoes, basil, cheese, nuts and garlic in a food processor or blender and blend.

2. While motor is running, add olive oil in a steady stream until blended.

3. Add salt and pepper to taste.

Tapanade

This easy-to-make crowd pleaser can be used as a dip, pasta sauce, or as a topping for pizza or Bruschetta.

1/2 cup Pimento stuffed green olives

1/2 cup pitted Kalamata olives

2 tablespoons capers, drained

2 cloves garlic, minced

1/4 cup extra virgin olive oil

1/2 teaspoon black pepper

1. Add all ingredients to the food processor and pulse until ingredients form a coarse relish consistency.

Chicken Stock

Homemade stock is worth the time and effort. You can make a big batch and freeze it, either in quart-size containers or in ice cube trays to make handy stock cubes that you can pop into recipes for added flavor.

1 chicken (about 4 pounds), cut in quarters

4 quarts water

2 onions, peeled and quartered

4 stalks celery, roughly chopped

3 carrots, peeled and roughly chopped

4 sprigs fresh parsley

2 bay leaves

4 sprigs fresh thyme

1 tablespoon salt

1 teaspoon whole peppercorns, or 1/2 teaspoon ground black pepper

1. Add all ingredients to a 6-8 quart stock pot. Gently bring to a boil over medium high heat.

2. Once the stock comes to a boil reduce heat and simmer, uncovered for about 2-1/2 hours.

3. Strain stock through a colander or strainer lined with cheesecloth. Refrigerate up to 3 days or freeze until ready to use.

Marinara Sauce

We've used this sauce in our lasagnas, eggplant Parmesan, chicken Parmesan and many different pasta dishes. We add cooked Italian sausage to it as a meat sauce option when we serve thousands of hungry triathletes at the annual Wildflower Festival in May at Lake San Antonio.

1/4 cup olive oil

1/4 cup fresh garlic, minced

2 onions chopped

1 bell pepper, chopped

2 stalks celery, finely chopped

3, 28-ounce cans tomato sauce

2, 28-ounce cans diced tomatoes

1/2 cup good red wine

1 tablespoon salt

1/2 tablespoon black pepper

1 tablespoon Italian seasoning

1 teaspoon dried whole oregano

1/2 teaspoon dried thyme leaves

1 teaspoon dried basil or 1/2-ounce fresh basil leaves, chopped

1. Heat oil in a 4- to 6-quart stock pot over medium heat.

2. Add garlic and onions. Cook, stirring until soft, about 2-3 minutes. Add bell pepper, celery, and cook for an additional 2 minutes. Add tomato sauce, diced tomatoes, red wine, and seasonings.

3. Reduce heat and simmer, uncovered, for about 2 hours.

4. Cool and refrigerate up to 5 days or freeze in portions you will use later.

Enchilada Sauce

This is the secret to our Enchiladas (page 122), but it can also be used as a base for other dishes such as Chile Colorado or a Mexican-inspired beef stew. You will have enough sauce for a couple of pans of enchiladas. The sauce will hold in the refrigerator for up to a week and it freezes well.

1/2 pound unsalted butter

3/4 cup all purpose flour

2 quarts warm stock, chicken, beef or vegetable

1/2 cup chili powder

1 ounce pasilla chili powder

2 teaspoons salt

2 teaspoons granulated garlic

2 teaspoons dried oregano

1 teaspoon black pepper

1 teaspoon ground cumin

1/4 teaspoon crushed red pepper

1/8 teaspoon ground cinnamon

1. Melt butter in a medium saucepan. When the butter is melted, whisk in flour. Cook the roux, stirring frequently, for about 5 minutes.

2. Whisk in warm stock. Add the remaining ingredients and simmer over medium heat until it thickens. The sauce should be the consistency of heavy cream. If the sauce seems too thick you can thin it with a little more stock or water.

Marinated Feta & Olives

This is a very versatile condiment. I use it in antipasto and it is great mixed into pasta salad or tossed into Warm Arugula Pesto Pasta (page 84).

1 pound feta cheese, crumbled

1 cup sliced green olives

1 cup sliced Kalamata olives

1 cup extra virgin olive oil

1 tablespoon chopped fresh garlic

2 teaspoons chopped fresh rosemary

1 tablespoon chopped fresh oregano

1/2 teaspoon crushed red pepper

1/4 teaspoon ground black pepper

1. Mix all the ingredients together and let marinate for at least 4 hours. Store in the refrigerator for up to 2 weeks.

Marinated Fresh Mozzarella

I can make a meal out of this with fresh baguettes or crostinis. Fresh Mozzarella typically comes in 4-ounce balls or "bocconcini," which are also called "cherry size," and either will work for this recipe.

4, 4-ounce fresh
mozzarella balls, cut into
1/4-inch slices, or 1 pound
bocconcini

1/4 cup fresh basil, chopped

1/2 cup extra virgin olive oil

2 tablespoons
white balsamic vinegar

2 cloves garlic, minced

1 teaspoon coarse salt

1/2 teaspoon fresh ground
black pepper

1/4 teaspoon crushed red
pepper flakes

1 Put the fresh mozzarella in a medium glass or stainless bowl.

2. In a separate bowl, mix together the remaining ingredients and pour over the mozzarella.

3. Cover and refrigerate for at least 4 hours or overnight, stirring 2 or 3 times. Serve with sliced French bread or crostini.
Serves 4-6

Homemade Croutons

When we had the restaurant we used our leftover day-old bread to make our croutons. We use primarily San Luis Sourdough bread for our croutons although any bread will do.

**8 tablespoons butter
(1 stick)**

1 tablespoon granulated garlic

2 tablespoons parsley flakes

**2 quarts cubed bread
(about 8 cups)**

1/2 cup Parmesan cheese, grated

1. Preheat oven to 325 degrees F.

2. Melt butter in a small saucepan. Stir in garlic and parsley flakes.

3. Place cubed bread in a medium bowl. Pour butter mixture over bread and mix well. Add Parmesan cheese; stir again to coat well.

4. Spread mixture onto a baking sheet and bake for about 60 minutes, stirring every 15 minutes until the croutons start to brown and crisp.
    8 cups

Wasabi Aioli

1 clove garlic, finely chopped

1 egg

2 tablespoons lemon juice

1 tablespoon wasabi paste

1/2 cup each canola oil
and mild olive oil (or 1 cup
canola/olive oil blend)

1/2 teaspoon salt

1. Add the garlic, egg, lemon juice, and wasabi to the bowl of the food processor fitted with the steel blade. Blend for about 5 seconds.

2. With the motor running slowly begin adding the oil, in a slow stream, until it is incorporated and thick, about the consistency of mayonnaise.

If you don't want to go to the trouble of making aioli, or are concerned about the raw egg, you can substitute 3/4 cup of commercial, store-bought mayonnaise for the egg.

NOTE: Raw egg preparations are generally considered safe for healthy adults, when handled with care. See page 171 for safe egg handling practices.

Index

CAHOOTS COOKBOOK

Table of Equivalents

LIQUID MEASUREMENTS:
Dash = 2-4 drops
1/2 cup = 1/8 quart = 1/4 pint = 4 fluid ounces
1 cup = 1/4 quart = 1/2 pint = 8 fluid ounces
2 cups = 1/2 quart = 1 pint = 16 fluid ounces
4 cups = 1/4 gallon = 1 quart = 2 pints = 32 fluid ounces
8 cups = 1/2 gallon = 2 quarts = 4 pints = 64 fluid ounces
16 cups = 1 gallon = 4 quarts = 8 pints = 128 fluid ounces

DRY MEASUREMENTS
1/16 cup = 1 tablespoon = 3 teaspoons = 15 milliliters
1/8 cup = 2 tablespoons = 6 teaspoons = 30 milliliters
1/4 cup = 4 tablespoons = 12 teaspoons = 50 milliliters
1/3 cup = 5 1/3 tablespoons = 16 teaspoons = 75 milliliters
1/2 cup = 8 tablespoons = 24 teaspoons = 125 milliliters
2/3 cup = 10 2/3 tablespoons = 32 teaspoons = 150 milliliters
3/4 cup = 12 tablespoons = 36 teaspoons = 175 milliliters
1 cup = 16 tablespoons = 48 teaspoons = 250 milliliters

TO CONVERT COOKING TIMES FOR CONVECTION OVENS:
Either lower the oven temperature by 25 degrees (long cooking, covered dishes may require reducing by as much as 50 degrees), or check the food about 3/4 of the way through the original cooking time.

Use the test your recipe gives you for doneness (*i.e.* internal temperature), and do not rely solely on appearance.

WINE MEASUREMENTS:

375 milliliters = 1/2 standard bottle

750 milliliters = 1 standard bottle

946 milliliters = 1 U.S. quart

1.5 liters = Magnum = 2 standard bottles

3 liters – Double Magnum = 4 standard bottles

1 U.S. gallon = 5 standard bottles

4.5 liters – Jeroboam = 6 standard bottles

6 liters = Imperial or Methuselah = 8 standard bottles

9 liters = Salmanzar = 12 standard bottles

12 liters = Balthazar – 16 standard bottles

15 liters = Nebuchadnezzar = 20 standard bottles

Raw Egg Warning: Some health officials have advised that eating raw or undercooked meat, poultry, eggs or seafood poses a health risk to everyone, and it has been suggested that the risk is greater for the elderly, children under age 4, pregnant women and other highly susceptible individuals with compromised immune systems. Otherwise healthy people still need to remember that there is a risk and treat eggs and other raw animal foods accordingly. Thorough cooking of such animal foods reduces the risk of illness.

There have been specific advisories against consuming raw or lightly cooked eggs on the grounds that the egg may be contaminated with Salmonella, a bacterium responsible for a type of food poisoning. Use only properly refrigerated, clean, sound-shelled, fresh, grade AA or A eggs, and avoid mixing yolks and whites with their shell. Consumers who want more information should contact their physician or local health department.

GO TO
www.cahootscatering.com
to order:
Chipotle Mayonnaise
Chipotle Sauce
House Rub
Thai Salad Dressing

Valentine's Dinner, Opolo Winery, February 14, 2007